# RABBI ISAAC JACOB REINES
## His LIFE and THOUGHT

# RABBI ISAAC JACOB REINES
## His LIFE and THOUGHT

*by* JOSEPH WANEFSKY

PHILOSOPHICAL LIBRARY
New York

Copyright © 1970, by PHILOSOPHICAL LIBRARY, INC.
15 East 40th St., New York, N. Y. 10016

Library of Congress Catalog Card No. 79-118314
SBN 8022-2349-4

Published by Philosophical Library, Inc.
*Manufactured in United States of America*

# Contents

*Introduction* .................................................. 1

I PSYCHOLOGY OF THE SPIRIT OF THE INDIVIDUAL
  AND THE NATION .............................. 5

II VIEWS ON MAN'S SPIRITUAL DEVELOPMENT ............ 37

III VIEWS ON JEWISH EDUCATION ...................... 76

IV IDEAS ON ZIONISM ................................ 129

*Selected Bibliography* ............................. 171

# ACKNOWLEDGMENTS

I would like to express my sincere gratitude and heartfelt appreciation to all those who have assisted and encouraged me to attain my doctoral degree. The consistent devotion and continuous encouragement that I have received from Drs. Samuel Belkin and Emanuel Rackman will be forever cherished as a symbol of helpful guidance.

Dr. Lander and Mrs. Kardon of the Bernard Revel Graduate School have always expressed their kind consideration and helpful cooperation to ameliorate any problem that arose during the course of my work. To my doctoral committee goes my sincere appreciation for their dedicated assistance.

My dear and personal friend, Dr. Jacob Jay Lindenthal, of Yale University, assisted me with many helpful suggestions. I am privileged and honored by his devoted friendship and dedicated comradeship.

I wish to thank the various organizations who have contributed their services to me during my course of study. The Hebrew Braille Association, The Lighthouse for The Blind, Recordings for the Blind and The Hadassah Women have all contributed reader assistance during my doctoral program at Yeshiva University.

To the many students of Yeshiva University and to the members of the B'nei Akiva Group of Washington Heights, New York, I owe a special debt of gratitude for their diligent and consistent reading. I am forever grateful to the Sol and Lillian Ash Foundation for their munificent assistance.

Rabbi Herschel Schachter, who has devoted his creative ability to the welfare and security of the American Jewish community, also has a profound awareness of the personal aspirations of the individual. Through his gifted dynamic leadership, the Mizrachi Organization has enhanced its intellectual and cultural dignity. It is my privilege to have received his kind assistance and consideration.

I would also like to express my deep gratitude and appreciation to Mr. Louis A. Pincus, Chairman of the Executive of the Jewish Agency, for his generous help and gracious cooperation in advancing the publication of this manuscript.

RABBI ISAAC JACOB REINES
His LIFE and THOUGHT

# Introduction

Rabbi Isaac Jacob Reines was born into an illustrious family in the year 1840. Rabbi Shlomoh Naphtali, his father, was one of the early pioneers who settled in Israel at the beginning of the 19th century. Because of various misfortunes, Rabbi Shlomoh Naphtali could not remain in Israel. While traveling in Poland he learned that his business and family were destroyed owing to an earthquake in Israel. He then resettled in Poland and remarried. The son born of this marriage was named Isaac Jacob.

Isaac Jacob studied in the Yeshiva of Volozhin and there he became known as a young prodigy. He devoted his time and energy to Torah and then assumed several pulpit positions, his most important one being at Lida. There he blossomed forth into a renowned religious figure.

Isaac Jacob was both a rosh yeshiva and a religious leader, the head of an academy and a leader of his people. Reines as we know was inspired in his revolutionary creative life and thought by two mainstreams of thought. He had a rich, cultural heritage nurtured and developed in an illustrious home where he was inspired by his father with the burning desire for the love of Torah. He was also trained in Volozhin, the leading academy of Jewish spiritual learning. We note the interesting and provocative stages in the intellectual development of Reines. He studied the logical treatise of the Rambam and was impressed by the geometry of Euclid. He also read Sholem Aleichem who he thought was a *letz*, a jester. Reines was able to discern between those secular strands that tend to assimilate and those secular ideas that pull together and are intertwined with the sacred. He was a man inspired with the idea of reviving the cultural atrophy of his people for the rebirth of Israel but was also acquainted with the plight of his brethren in the Diaspora. He was the man of *regesh*. Reines wrote constantly about his philosophy of *regesh*, history based upon *regesh*, the emotive quality within man and the nation which gives rise to the development of great principles. However he knew that this idea of reawakening the spirit through *regesh* must be coupled and nurtured with *sechel*, the rational qualities of man. They cannot be severed; they must be interrelated.

The Yeshiva of Lida which he led was perhaps a forerunner of our own Yeshiva University and was the archetype of synthesizing and interrelating the secular with the sacred. His bold and dynamic plan was perhaps far removed from the immediate range of that communal planning because the Jews in the European community were not keen about his new venture. He did meet, however, with moderate success. We have been able to transplant his ideas upon new soil within our own diasporic conditions.

This idea of the new modern Yeshiva in Lida evoked various types of responses as we will discuss in the articles which follow. Lida had a yeshiva wherein not only the intellectual, creative, analytical sections of the Talmud were studied but also wherein much time was devoted to the ethical, to Tenach, Grammar, and various subjects pertaining to the Torah. It was a yeshiva designed to inculcate the yearning student with an identity of his tradition and to fortify him with a protective shield against the external pressures of the secular culture and the internal disintegration of the Jewish community resulting from pogroms and other persecutions.

The Lida Yeshiva was a dynamic new venture that was a product of Reines' own personal development, a yeshiva in which creative intellectual study was combined with the ethical purview of traditional Judaism. The Yeshiva of Lida and the religious Zionist movement were his main creative contributions. They demonstrate his ability to be the rosh yeshiva who was aware of the students' yearning needs and their intellectual necessities. Reines was also aware of the need of future generations

—that they would require a resting place, an established eternal homeland in Israel. He was cognizant of both the needs of the present and those of the future simultaneously, of the intellectual youth and the adult layman. His perception of the problems of his age was both penetrating and intuitive.

Reines was created from the tragedy of the earthquake in 1840 and died amidst the turmoil of the First World War. His personal and communal environment inspired him with a deep-seated feeling for his brethren. As we have mentioned before, he was acclaimed and criticized by the secular Jewish society and the radical orthodox right. He championed steadfastly his ideas in the face of all opposition. He was aware of the fact that he was a rebel, for at 60 years he assumed the helm of leadership for the new religious Zionist movement. As an older rabbi, he could have served complacently in his pulpit. Reines did not need to become the fearless leader encompassed with the harsh criticism of his peers. Yet he asserted himself and assumed the challenge of understanding his people and leading them in the movement to safeguard the torch of Judaism for future generations. He had a great influence upon Rabbi Kook and many future Zionist leaders.

He was the polemicist, the man endowed with great intellectual and spiritual energy, the man who was gifted in presenting an argument, for in his time this was necessary to prepare the groundwork for future generations. His was the revolutionary type of mind. Reines was a man who was not to be overly influenced by the static conservative approach of traditional thinking. Therefore, my interpretation of the articles which follow tend to illustrate the character of Reines and express his thought in the various chapters concerning human development, education and Zionism. The life and thought of a man are inseparable. They are inextricably intertwined. Thus Reines is extremely important for his singular contribution to creative Jewish thought. He understood his past and had a concern for the future. He was aware of the entire panorama of Judaism. His life was dedicated to the intellectual and creative development of his people and to securing the safety and well-being of his nation. He must be studied because his life symbolizes the Jew in transition, the Jew who can synthesize and mold his character at all times and in all periods. He is the Jew who can bridge the past and the future within his own particular frame of reference.

# 1

# Psychology of the Spirit of the Individual and the Nation

Dr. Hirsch Leib Gordon has endeavored to share some of his recollections of Rabbi Reines depicting his portrait in the category of rosh yeshiva and *godol hador*. Reines was considered a public figure and subjected to criticism by various factions and groups of Jews. The Chassidim decried his short jacket which was worn only by western Europeans. They also considered him unshaven although he had a long beard. The assimilationists criticized him for his overzealous activities in the advent of the Zionist movement. The orthodox Jews were not to be denied their share of criticism for his irreverent approach concerning the Messianic tradition. Upon promulgating his plan for organizing a religious wing within the construct of the Zionist movement, Reines met adverse opposition from many religious leaders. Although Rav Yitzchak Elchanan and the *N'tziv* of Wolozin were interested in the idea of reviving a love for Zion, *N'tziv* could hardly agree to the revolutionary approach purported by Reines. Reines, however, did not succumb to the conservative appeal by many scholars and laymen to abdicate his position and forego his interest toward establishing religious Zionism. Gordon complains that Reines has been almost completely forgotten for the role that he played concerning this great movement.[1]

Gordon relates that when he was a child he would ask his

---

[1] H. L. Gordon, "Rabbi Isaac Jacob Reines," *Hadoar*, (March, 1965), p. 304.

father or other rabbis whom they considered to be the three greatest men of our generation. They could never ignore Reines for his unique knowledge in all facets of Jewish culture. Although on all public notices where the *gedolim* would sign, the name of Reines was absent, and yet no one could deny his unique genius and great scholarship in Torah. Reines would not submit to the unanimity of the *gedolim* for upholding the *status quo* concerning the communal life of European Jewry. He always maintained that we are not like all the nations at large. We have our own destiny to fulfill harmonizing the truth of religion with the spirit of nationalism. In many of Reines' books, he has incorporated the term *or*—light as a symbol of his desire to imbue and illuminate his readers with his original ideas concerning the problems of Judaism. His books on *drush* are completely devoted to the issues of his time and to the problems of his age. Rabbi Reines had an unusual appeal as a leader in the eyes of his students who were devoted to his cause and inspired by his dynamic qualities of leadership. Reines, therefore, appears as a religious political leader and also as a teacher within the scope of traditional yeshiva life. In his new approach, Reines aimed to contribute within the methodology of comprehending and appreciating the treasure of principles: That is, to be explored within the corpus of Jewish law. (He attempted to convey this in his classic works.) He had many associates who collaborated with him in launching the new movement. At his side were many great Jewish contemporaries namely Rabbi Abraham I. Kook, Rabbi Elyah Gutmacher, Rabbi Nahum Greenhaus, Rabbi Yehudah Dun Yichyeh, Rabbi Pinchas Rozhnitsky and Rabbi Shmuel Yaacov Rabinowitz. There were also two great literary personalities who were involved in developing the nucleus of the movement namely Rav Zev Yavitz and Abraham Yaacov Slutsky who, incidentally, coined the movement with its name—Mizrachi. These men were naturally instrumental in the cause of creating religious Zionism. Reines, however, was the key figure and the prime mover who gave the incentive and impetus to proceed along the course that would recreate and rejuvenate the Jewish community. He was eager to be incorporated within the curriculum a new appreciation for Jewish nationalism. Unlike the other yeshivas who were merely preoccupied with Talmudic pilpul, he endeavored to inspire his students with all facts of Jewish culture.[2]

In the Yeshiva of Lida, Tenach was studied. A knowledge of Hebrew Grammar and Hebrew Literature was also required as a necessary part of the educational program. The youth thereby would grow to appreciate and be inculcated with an interest that would inspire and develop their love for the Jewish nation as well as for its academic learning. Rabbi Reines was also accustomed to deliver a sermon every Friday evening after dinner. No matter how thick the snow fell during the long cold dark winter night he would step quickly through the streets rushing to deliver his Friday evening lecture. Dr. Gordon describes how a student would accompany him along the way that he, too, was so fortunate to have enjoyed that privilege in the year 1910. Gordon proceeds to demonstrate how Reines developed the structure of his lecture on a particular topic. The *shiur* concerned the laws of witnesses. Reines asked why if a group of three witnesses come to testify about a case in question concerning capital punishment we declare that if one is found to give invalid testimony then the entire group becomes nullified. However, when we compare this concept in relation to monetary laws, we note that if one witness shall testify without due validity then the testimony of the remaining two witnesses shall prevail to uphold the case. Reines then proceeds to distinguish between these two categories of testimony, namely, capital laws and monetary laws. The witnessing of capital laws is a partnership that is governed by an organic relationship. If one witness shall testify invalidly then he has destroyed the entire unit for he is a part of an organic relationship and the entire group has thereby surrendered its validity. However, concerning monetary witnessing the group consists of a mechanical relationship and if one testimony is held to be invalid it does not necessarily disqualify the entire group for in this case his testimony is not crucial to the formation of the witnessing part-

---

[2] *Ibid.*, p. 305.

nership. Therefore, we can differentiate between the requirement governing monetary laws and those of capital laws.

This idea that Gordon relates about Reines is not an isolated thought nor is it strange to his total conceptual scheme. It demonstrates, moreover, the primary concern within his scope of thinking. Reines is constantly preoccupied with the organic structure rather than the mechanical form of Judaism. It is the organic unit that gives expression and vitality to inspire and develop the intellectual and creative Judaism to which he devoted all his life with vigorous energy and dynamic insight.[3]

Reines discussed his ideas concerning the return to the love for Zion. He raised his voice and cried with bitter anguish and deep remorse over the separation of the people of Israel from their homeland. This was not a lament like that in the Yeshiva of Slobodka during the penitential month of Ellul. His was a cry and plea for the salvation and redemption of the entire nation to become completely restored as of old. It was not the Slobodka cry of personal penitence—it was rather the wailing of the universal national expression that was a unique experience for the Lida students. Reines was diligent in his pursuit of Torah study. With the rise of the morning star one would find him bent over his books with pen in hand pouring out his intellectual, creative and imaginative work with prolific and industrious speed. At night, one could see him pouring out his tears over the great destruction and colossal ruin that had befallen our national pride.

Rabbi Meyer Berlin, in his classic work *From Wolozin to Jerusalem,* gives us an account of the Lida Yeshiva and its founder, Rabbi Reines. According to Berlin, Rabbi Reines had nurtured for a long time the idea of establishing a yeshiva with a unique program even while he was a rabbi in Shvinzin in the 1880's. He had decided on a revolutionary experiment in creating a model yeshiva. However, it did not come to fruition until he became rabbi in Lida. Only after his name had become more popular within the circles of rabbinic scholars and en-

---

[3] *Ibid.,* p. 306.

lightened Jews did he seize upon the opportunity to fulfill his plan.[4]

Rabbi Berlin was not too enthusiastic about this new yeshiva. He declared that this new revolutionary venture of creating an ideal type yeshiva would never reach its projected glory. Those who thought that it would be highly secularized with a new view of modernity became greatly disappointed with its ties to the traditional Talmudic learning. Reines' contemporaries underestimated him greatly, hence the fame of his yeshiva suffered immensely. Many religious leaders did not appreciate the great scholarship and deep piety with which Reines was endowed. Berlin contends that he ranked among the greatest of his generation. The Maskilim or enlightened Jews were also disillusioned for Reines was neither more *makal* nor less *machmir* in any particular *halacha* than his contemporaries. Also if one were to come to Lida at any time during the late hours of the night, he would find Reines absorbed in his study and immersed in writing his *Chidush* Torah. Why then was he considered to be a liberal in the eyes of the religious rightists? Two characteristics of his style of writing gave rise to mistrust of his character. His unique style of writing that presupposed a revolutionary method incurred the enmity of the rabbis. He also had an unusual drive towards exerting his intellectual curiosity that led one to believe that he was advancing something new, something foreign to the views of orthodox Judaism.

It can be said that Reines advanced a new method in delivering sermons and expositing homiletical *midrashim*. With logic and warmth, he cultivated his unique style in an effort to inspire and motivate his listeners to the problems of his age. Unlike the other *darshanim* Reines was concerned with the issues prevalent in his time. He was not concerned with petty details or lofty ideas. Rather his concern was to express his views on a problem that was intrinsically vital to the whole Jewish community. His books on *drush* demonstrate his capacity for presenting a problem and analyzing it to its minute and definitive concepts.

---

[4] Meyer Berlin, *From Wolozin to Jerusalem*, (Tel Aviv: Yalkut, 1939), II, p. 231.

The Lida Yeshiva was also gifted with the presence of the Maitcheter Illui. Reines was particularly fond of having such a leading intellectual figure in his academy. Many other yeshivas would have been proud to include the Illui as a lecturer on their faculties.[5]

Rabbi Berlin was impressed with Reines' preoccupation in practical Judaism. Reines was extremely perplexed when the Jewish community was confronted with serious tragedy and grave problems. He always remarked—What can we do to alleviate the situation? How can we remedy the plight of our brethren? Why aren't the other leaders doing something or using their influence to help the cause of Judaism? He had a burning desire for the love of his people and his whole life was dedicated to enhance the glory of Jewry.

The experiment of the Lida Yeshiva, although coming to an untimely end, interrupted by both the First World War and the death of its leader, contributed greatly to the advancement of the Jewish community. It was an attempt or at least an experimental yeshiva that evoked the dual concept within the life of a yeshiva student. It was, as has been noted, the great forerunner of our own Yeshiva University, the picture model of harmonizing and blending all facets of life within the framework of the young aspiring Torah student. The infant stage of Lida did not materialize to its full potential because of the problems that were unique to its geographical locale, pressures exerted by certain rabbis and perhaps the limited funds. Nevertheless, the ideal of the yeshiva was transplanted to a new locale. Its program was adopted and adapted to our own American Jewish community. The vision of an innovator always meets with great stress and great conflict.[6]

Yeshaiah Wolfsberg attempts to compare and contrast Reines and Rabbi Kook. Both fought valiantly and courageously for the resurrection of Jewish national pride and the resettlement of our forsaken homeland. Both were also dynamic in their intellectual creativity. The other *gedolim* of their age either did not measure up to them in scholarship or lacked their devotion

---

[5] *Ibid.*, p. 232.   [6] *Ibid.*, p. 233.

and dedication for the resettlement of a Jewish homeland. Reines and Kook were endowed with the unique capability of harmonizing within their conceptual scheme the people and the law. The people and the law were inexorably intertwined and one could not exist without the other. Although Rabbi Kook inherited the helm of Zionist leadership from Rabbi Reines and he survived him for nearly a generation, he nevertheless was still considered a contemporary and we may justly compare and distinguish between the two. Reines had a natural and innate love for Israel that was ingrained in his soul. Although he himself was unable to realize his dreams of settling in Israel his father who had settled there and who was forced to leave because of the fortuitous event instilled his son with the burning desire and kindled within him the flame of Zionism. Rabbi Kook on the other hand arrived at his convictions by his own motivation. He dreamed and longed for Israel and at an early age. We may, therefore, contrast the two in these terms. Reines' behavior toward Israel was almost biologically hereditary while with Rabbi Kook it was a creative romantic experience that imbued him with the drive for the establishment of Israel. Paradoxically, however, Reines' chief accomplishments were beyond the boundaries of Israel while Kook's creative contribution was within Israel proper. Reines fought the battle of vindicating and championing the Zionist ideal against the right-wing orthodox who were content with the status quo. Kook, however, was a passionate man who sought to persuade and impress those who were irreligious within the scope of a truly Torah Zionism. Both Reines and Kook wrote works on *drush* and *halacha*. Both were endowed and gifted with the unique perception and keen observation of the totality in Jewish culture. However, it may be said that Reines employed within his system the intellectual and analytical approach establishing his theories as geometrical axioms and propositions that were either proven or disproven. Kook's philosophical system was intrinsically romantic in nature and metaphysical in structure.[7]

---

[7] Y. O. Wolfsberg, "Two Great Luminaries of Mizrachi," Introduction.

In Reines, we see a man with a burning energetic zeal, a man who was fighting and waging war to uphold his belief and opinions. In Kook, we see a man filled with a passionate love and a gentle personal glow who had the gift of tolerance in conveying his ideas to his followers. The term *or*—light—is a predominant element in the books of both Reines and Kook imbuing the readers with the incandescent spirituality that transmits an inner glow and an external splendor for a vibrant and dynamic interpretation of Judaism.

There is another article that sheds light on the character and personality of Rabbi Reines. "Rabbi Moshe Shmuel Shapiro and His Generation," a book of essays depicts the life of some luminaries of the rabbinic world during the 19th and 20th centuries.[8]

Accordingly Rabbi Reines was named after his mother's family called Reines. Although many sought to view him as an extremely cultured man and also as a political figure, he retained his typical European rabbinical stature. Despite the fact that he never immersed himself in the enlightenment literature he was not estranged from it. Reines would remark concerning Sholem Aleichem that he was a *letz*, a jester, however, an extremely gifted cynic—*baal kishron*. He was neither influenced nor in ecstasy about Sholem Aleichem nor was he exceptionally impressed with Bialik. Reines would declare that if one is interested in deriving pleasure from poetry he should immerse himself in our ancient literature, namely the homiletical passages in our *midrashim* and *yalkutim*. Reines had a unique talent for grasping the spirit of the times and the problems of Judaism that were confronted by it. He remarked that he was only opening a door, for the throbbing problems of history demand a new reevaluation of our academic system.

If we let the constant stirrings of the secularized clamor continue then decay shall set in and the foundations of Judaism, the edifice that was established until now shall, G-d Forbid, become destroyed. We must, therefore, introduce a program

---

[8] Moshe S. Shapiro, *Rabbi Moshe Shmuel Shapiro and His Generation*, p. 18.

that shall give guidance, direction and proper instruction to our youth if we are to develop a vigorous Jewry that will confront the problems of our age with the perspective of our heritage.[9]

Rabbi Reines had engaged the financial support of many leading Russian Jewish philanthropists in order to secure the funds necessary for providing the upkeep of his yeshiva. Such great notables as Baron Ginsburg and the Wisotsky family were among the many generous contributors to his yeshiva. Reines who was gifted as a public speaker was quite different from the other *darshanim*. His sermons would arouse and inspire the soul and the spirit of his listeners. He did not engage himself in an intellectual exercise that would be entertaining for his audience. When he gave a sermon, he was completely involved with the plight of his brethren and the pride of his nation. There were many followers who absorbed the unique style and gifted expression from the sermons of Rabbi Reines. He was a source of inspiration to many a public speaker and his books served as a model for conveying the immediate problems of the age at the pulpit. Within his pen there fused a profound analytical and concise logic coupled with the warm and animated style which motivated men to become overwhelmed and transformed by his writings.

Rabbi Shapiro appraised Reines' ingenious writings and hastened to add that Reines was too far advanced for his age. He had developed a style that was unique and original in both its form and content. The designated projects *Chosem Tochnis, Adus B'yaakov,* and *Orim Gedolim* were too revolutionary for students and even for rabbis who were routinized in the path of the old rabbinic style of pilpul. However, he was hailed among those groups of scholars who were concerned with systemizing and organizing the study of the Talmud on a scientific plane. Reines' *drashot* we have noted previously gripped the pulse of his people and enhanced the position of the pulpit. He expressed himself that the sermonizer must be attuned to the plight of his people. As a father assists his young and aids the

---

[9] Isaac Jacob Reines, *Shnei Hamoros,* (Pyetrokov, Russia: S. Belechovsky, 1913), II, p. 52.

child in walking, similarly must the rabbi be the helpmate to encourage and uplift his congregation. Spiritual emotion and devotion for the law are the spinal cord and the nucleus of his intellectual creativity. He exclaimed many times that he had all but become disillusioned from being involved in any group activity. However the angel of *regesh* engulfed his personality and transformed his character to realize always the need and urgency of being involved in communal activities.[10]

We have stated before the dual role within the scope of Reines' achievements, namely, as rosh yeshiva and founder of the Mizrachi movement. His awareness of the unique problems of his age can be seen through his many works on theological problems. Here, however, we will briefly cite a few passages from his writings, demonstrating his keen concern for what he considered important. About the formation of a new type yeshiva he writes:

> From my youth till today I have not diverted my gaze for a moment from the camp of Israel and from every development on the Jewish scene, however small, and I have investigated the root of everything and its latter end. For many years my daily experience has confirmed the bitter and horrible truth that the Torah is becoming a dead letter and that our youth are becoming estranged. I visualized this dreadful picture as early as forty years ago and foresaw the danger in store which has now fully materialized. Even then I saw our houses of study destined to become empty and our children straying onto other worlds; our Torah in a corner and our youthful commonwealth devoid of a knowledge of Judaism and the slightest modicum of warm pure Hebrew feeling. With what are we confronted today? Have not these prognostications been fulfilled in the most dreadful manner? Where is the Torah mastery which distinguished the previous generation? Where are our children, our hope for the future and where are they pasturing? Where is the great love for the people and its sacred traditions, the selfless dedication to them that pervaded our fathers' beings? Our children have forsaken us and there is no one to inherit that wonderful legacy bequeathed to us from the days of yore. Why has this catastrophe overtaken

---

[10] *Ibid.*, p. 53.

us, the likes of which has never been in Israel? What is the source of this calamity? I answered this terrible question thirty years ago. We are to blame. I then asserted that so long as we have no college which provide a combination of Jewish and general knowledge, introducing some of the beauty of Japhet into the tents of Shem, equipping Torah scholars with general culture, till then there is no hope of preventing our children seeking a refuge in other fields. The forces of our environment are too strong and only a few will be able to resist them and succeed. Life has changed in recent times so radically, causing a revolution in the world of the Jew. The old must adjust itself a little to the new needs. Our houses of study must take on somewhat of a new appearance so as not to lose out on their historic role and continue to attract our youth. Only such colleges which, besides providing their students with a thorough and comprehensive mastery of the Torah, will equip them in other subjects too, can ensure rearing a generation loyal to their G-d and their people. I gave utterance to such sentiments then in the presence of all the spiritual leaders of our people and called on them to rise up whilst there was yet time and anticipate the evil. But my voice was as one crying in the wilderness. The danger was still not apparent, and no one listened to me. Then I took the initiative and went alone into the fray and built my first yeshiva at Shvensin. But the internal and external obstacles were too great and my first venture fizzled out for want of support. Thirty years passed by bringing with them the troubles I had foreseen and drawing us nearer to the abyss which threatened to swallow up our sons and daughters. But at the same time those thirty years, the beginnings of Zionist settlement, pogroms, Herzl, etc., wrought a radical change in men's minds. That which had appeared strange became obvious and essential now. Others came to my conclusions and then I founded the great yeshiva in Lida.[11]

Reines also viewed the newly created movement of Zionism as a bulwark for stemming the tide of rising assimilation. He contended that the movement would prevent the dissolution of the Jewish community from its impending peril when confronted by those nations who sought to destroy it. Then he

---

[11] Isaac Jacob Reines, "Mishkenoth Yaacov," *Jewish Life*, (January-February, 1966), pp. 21-25.

channeled his energy to foster a cohesive religious organic movement within the scope of Zionism. In his book, *Or Chodosh Al Zion,* he expressed his aim:

> Where there are people of different origins, outlook, and temperament there is almost bound to be dissension and opposing party groupings. [But no tribute is too high to pay for that ideal which succeeds in unifying divergent elements into a unified body.] The foregoing sentiments came to my mind when I attended my first Zionist Congress and when I saw that magnificent and awe-inspiring sight, that vast hall and lofty galleries full of people from different countries of divergent opinions, outlooks, and temperaments, all enthused by the common ideal of advancing the cause of the nation and its sacred homeland, to rebuild its ruins, and plant its deserts. When I saw this I said to myself, "How powerful is the attraction of Our Holy Land. How penetrating the comments of Rabbi Yehoshua ben Levi in the Talmud (Chagigah) on the verse (Ps. 121); Jerusalem that are built as a city that is compact together." A city that makes all Israel comrades together, the impact of whose holiness unites the Jews of such divergent outlooks and opinions.[12]

Michael Joseph Berditchevsky depicted Reines' character in a short biographical sketch. He calls Reines *Ish Haaschulot*—a man who is endowed with a multi-facet variety of knowledge—a man who was imbued with the totality of Jewish culture uniting on many varied subjects.[13] Reines was unlike the typical gadol—a great Jewish sage. He was perhaps one of the few of his generation who could speak out not only as a great Talmudist but also as a literari. In our times either the great Jewish personality is chiefly preoccupied and mainly concerned only with the Talmud and traditional pilpulistic way of learning or he is immersed in Haskalah—the literature that is confined to Jewish History, Philosophy, and Poetry. Briefly then we have two categories of scholarship that are a threat to the cohesion of the Jewish community. Moreover, they have incurred a large

---

[12] Isaac Jacob Reines, *Or Chodosh Al Zion,* (Vilna: Rom, 1902), pp. 3-28.
[13] M. J. Berditchevsky, "On Reines," *Otzer Hasifruth,* II (1888), pp. 228-234.

degree of schism within the rank and file of Jewish leadership. *Yisroel* and *Draita* have been torn asunder—the people and the law have been severed. Reines, however, sought to synthesize the two within his own conceptual scheme of understanding Jewish culture. He had the vision and the foresight to try and weld the two as the *chochmei seforat* of olden times. Reines in his new conception of analyzing Jewish law in his works *Chosem Tochnit*[14] and *Orim Geldim*[15] has demonstrated that Jewish laws are not isolated phenomena and detached details of infinite casuistry. He has, moreover, attempted to show that there is an underlying principle, a conceptual scheme and analytical framework that circumspects and navigates within the sea of the Talmud.

Rabbi Reines inspired by his universalistic approach desired to lead the Zionist movement to a new enlightened organization, *or chodosh*. He provided the incentive to others, namely Rabbi Kook, to grasp the enormous task that confronted the leaders of modern Jewry. Reines' intellectual approach was not circumscribed within the particular frame of reference that grows out of a narrow environment. He was rather imbued with a keen intuition that circumspects and extricates one from his particularistic view and transforms him into a being that is concerned with channeling and directing his people for a historic timeless task. This is the mission of the *manhig* and this was the ambition of Reines, to transform the diasporic mentality of the European Jew who was torn and throttled by the turmoil and torment of constant pogroms and continuing economic depression. Within Israel he saw and hoped for a new dream and even at times he was interested in resurrecting his people on the foreign soil of Uganda, however temporary that territory would have been, to replace the ever promised homeland of Israel. But this is the greatness of a leader who knows when and how to take the initiative however perilous it may appear. Now the true leader is bold and courageous, dynamic and daring. If one would contrast the characters of Reines and Kook, one would necessarily remain with this impression. Both wrote books with the title

---

[14] Isaac Jacob Reines, *Chosem Tochnit*, (Vilna: Rom, 1881).
[15] Isaac Jacob Reines, *Orim Gedolim*, (Vilna: Rom. 1886), pp. 1-18.

heading—*orah*—light. There is however a glaring distinction between them. Reines' light is drawn from a burning desire engulfed and enveloped with the issues of his time and the problems of his age. His light is a flame that comes from the nations of the world; nevertheless it is only a transitional state of affairs—that we shall overcome and the renaissance of Jewish glory shall once again reign throughout the earth.[16]

The Talmud relates that when Rabba was studying Torah, he was so immersed in his studies that even though his finger was bleeding, he did not feel any discomfort. This is to teach us that for the purpose of a higher pleasure of spiritualizing oneself the pain of physical torment evaporates. Physical torment becomes sublimated into spiritual satisfaction. The Jewish historical process has been one of sacrificing oneself and enduring persecution for a higher goal. We suffer in order to sanctify G-d's name. As Rabbi Meir of Rottenberg wrote: When the Jew experiences the act of martyrdom he does not feel any pain. The passage in Bamidbar Rabba also declares: *haraiti mori uvshami*. The *mor* meaning the suffering that the Jews have experienced throughout their historical travail has become a sweet smelling scent for we know that for Kiddush Hashem no sacrifice is too small.[17]

The feeling of one's personal dignity is a primary concept in Jewish theology. There are numerous citations in Talmud and Midrash elevating the idea of one's personal dignity. The virtue of modesty is a cardinal point in discerning the character of the Jewish nation. (We translate here the term *busha* as modesty.) He who is modest does not sin easily. Or as the Rabbis say that Jews may be discerned by three virtues—sympathy, modesty, and philanthropy. Now we may assert that the feeling of modesty arises from an inward dignity and personal pride of one's character. Hence, the realization of personal dignity is a cardinal point of distinction in each and every Jew. We know from historical fact that barbaric men are devoid of personal dignity because they lack the sensitivity that commands

---

[16] Isaac Jacob Reines, *Sefer Harochim* (New York: Publication Society, Inc., 1926), p. 65.
[17] *Ibid.*, p. 66.

self-respect. However, the human quality in man presupposes a sense of dignity, a torch that illuminates the path and gives direction to future generations, a light that arouses within man the raging desire to fight fierce battles and undertake a trailblazing and crusading path. This path is riddled with entrapments and the course of his road is extremely rugged. However, beyond the dismal darkness of our historic travail lies the glittering hope of a new light that will cast its rays on Zion and rekindle its people with a revived hope. Kook however was imbued with the flame that burns slowly and continually with all the love though quiet. Rabbi Kook was concerned with placating and calmly persuading the people to a zeal for Zion. Like the land of Israel adorned and attired with the beauty of its terrain and majestic territorial landscape, so was he a product of his environment. A religious personality that would transform the seething coals of Reines into the soft flame that would inspire his disciples. Thus Reines lit the torch giving direction within the religious camp to find the path toward their forgotten homeland.[18]

Yitzchak Gish Chalau relates that Reines was born into an illustrious family, a descendant of Saul Wahl. He was destined to become a leading Jewish figure fulfilling thereby a historic role. He was already hailed as a brilliant prodigy in his early boyhood years. He knew various tractates of the Talmud by heart and could recite them verbatim. When he was fifteen years old he had begun to pen his thoughts into a prolific stream of countless notations upon the Talmud. He had thereupon entered the Yeshiva of Wolozin and was extremely diligent in his studies, sleeping but two hours a night. His first major appointment to the pulpit was in the Town of Swieciany. There he assembled his writings in order to publish them. It was in Swieciany that Reines envisaged his plan to project a new and distinct methodology in the Talmud that would revolutionize its study. It was in Swieciany that Reines had embarked upon the plan of erecting his model type yeshiva. There, however,

---

[18] Y. O. Wolfsberg, "Two Great Luminaries of Mizrachi, *Or Hamizrach*," No. 3 (1956), Mizrachi Ha Poel Ha Mizrachi, New York.

his immediate plans were foiled and it had to take another two decades for him to realize his earlier dream. As we know, Reines was instrumental in establishing the religious wing within the cultural renaissance of the Zionist movement.[19]

At first Reines felt that Torah education should be separate and apart from political influence. However, when he saw that the secularists were intent upon inserting a cultural department within the movement then Reines at the fifth Congress of the Zionist movement established the idea of creating a religious educational concept of Zionism to maintain the orthodox point of view within the movement. As we know, Reines had decided to settle in Israel thereby culminating his lifetime dream. He wrote to Rabbi Judah Leib Hacohen Fishman that he was anxious to settle and make his home in the Holy Land. The First World War interrupted his plan for settlement and soon afterwards in 1915 he departed to his eternal rest. Because of bad communication due to the war, he was not eulogized properly. However, Israel recognized his greatness and named two settlements in his honor—Sde Yaacov in the valley of Jezreel; Nvai Yaacov in the suburbs of Jerusalem.

Reines was devoted and dedicated to communicating the sanctity and holiness of these phenomena, namely, the Torah, the land and the people. His creativity, therefore, can be expressed along three main branches of intellectual growth within Jewish literature. First, he was the expounder of new goals and new advances for a creative educational standard that would supersede previous generations and would serve the modern Jewish community as well. Then Reines was intent upon reviving and developing the political aspect of the Jewish community to realize for Israel a redemptive homeland that would be a refuge for all of Jewry in trying times. He was firmly convinced that he must understand and instruct his people toward the goal of developing their own character and personality, to inculcate them with the spirit of emotion and self-sacrifice that would demonstrate their unique individual capacity for with-

---

[19] *Ibid.*, p. 1-16.

standing and maintaining all pressures both internal and external.

Rabbi Maimon Fishman in his introduction to a reprint of *Eduth B'Yaacov*, a book on the laws of witnesses composed by Reines, presented a speech delivered by him concerning the platform of the Zionist movement.[20]

The political state, contended Reines, must be established upon religious principles. Religion is inexorably intertwined with state affairs. They cannot be made separate and apart. They must be integrated into one vibrant union. It is an old query—what determines history? Are the economic factors to be considered paramount or is the religious factor to be held supreme? If the economic factors are decisive in the development of general world history then Israel's fate of history is motivated by its religious and spiritual factors that infuse the people with their distinct characteristics. Israel has designated the spirit and the soul for the mission of its historic destiny. Church and state are not to be considered as isolated factors. They are, moreover, indivisible. Reines remarked that therein lay the distinction between the Jewish community and the world community.[21]

The world community can exist on a dual level system, namely, separation of church and state. The church and state of Israel's ideology spring forth from the realization of national survival. The Torah which is the essence of Judaism speaks in the same breath at one and the same time of an economic prosperity and spiritual compliance with G-d. You shall eat your bread satisfyingly and dwell upon your land in peace. No sword shall scorch your settlement and you shall pursue your enemies.[22] Then the statement follows that, I, G-d, shall reside within you. You shall be unto Me as a nation and I shall be unto you your G-d. Reines hastened to add that not only religious blessings associated with state blessings but also the religious curse of degradation is connected and linked up with political decadence and dissolution. Any Jew who lives beyond

---

[20] Isaac Jacob Reines, *Eduth B'Yaacov*, (Jerusalem: Mosad Harav Kook, 1951), pp. 5-11.
[21] *Ibid.*
[22] *Leviticus: 21.*

the borders of Israel is equivalent to one who worships idolatry. Israel when she is living in her homeland can best preserve her cultural identity and spiritual sovereignty. The birthplace and homeland of a nation is its container and protector. The preservation of Israel's cultural tradition requires a secure and safekeeping territory. "Whoever resides in Israel," remarks the Tosefta in Ketubahs, "is a G-dfearing man." The law of Israel has prescribed in its entirety not only laws that serve to regulate man's relation with G-d and his fellow man but also those laws that encompass the body politic of its nation. A further issue that would demonstrate the unity of purpose between Israel's religion and its state can be expressed within the context of another philosophical problem. Which precedes the other? Does the state create and form the religion? Or has the religion created and shaped for itself a state wherein religion should be viable?[23]

The Jewish state was created after it had received its model constitution, namely the Torah. If the Torah preceded governmental authority then we cannot say that Judaism had enjoyed a monarchy in its abstract sense. The king as we know from many passages in the Prophets was subjected on many occasions to rebuke. Hence the external or secular form of Judaism could not radically change the internal order of the Jewish community. We are not only a state that constitutes a composite of Jews but rather we are a Jewish state. The function of the Jewish government is not only to protect and secure the maintenance and order from without, namely against foreign intervention in incursion but it must assure its people internal peace and harmony by developing its cultural and social institutions. This lecture of Reines concerning the political structure of the preparation for the new Israel demonstrated once again his ability to fuse and weld the secular into the sacred. Reines had envisaged a political state that could operate within the framework of a religious system guided by the Torah. Inherent in Reines' approach was a universalistic conception of life seeking the harmony of all the elements to produce a viable political

---

[23] Isaac Jacob Reines, *Eduth B'Yaacov*, pp. 5-11.

structure. Reines' creativity was developed from an unusual set of circumstances. As related by Fishman, his father, Rabbi Shlomo Naftali, had already an established position of influence and affluence in the old Yishuv. However, circumstances—*hashgacha*—as it were had displaced the father from Israel. Rabbi Shlomo who was going on a mission to collect funds in Europe suddenly learned of the catastrophe that had befallen his family in the Holy Land. He had to resettle in the Diaspora and to rebuild his family life. Soon after the unfortunate event, he remarried and in the year 1840 a son was born to him. Isaac Jacob Reines was born into an environment of conflict. His maturity was placed against a background of struggling and striving for the complete dedication and ultimate devotion, and self-sacrifice and commitment to the ideal of Israel. The sociology of knowledge is the attempt to understand man's creativity which is derived from his environmental and hereditary influences. When we examine the total picture of Reines' creativity and contribution to the field of Jewish scholarship we must maintain this concept. The man was destined to develop new vistas in Jewish cultural life because he was cast into the cultural milieu by the titanic waves of his own personal life.[24]

Reines already was instilled with the eternal dream of returning to the promised land of Israel. While still a youth, Reines' desire was to fulfill his dream of experiencing a rejuvenated Judaism. However, it was not to be a Judaism based merely upon a natural territorial boundary line. This would, moreover, have to be placed within the scope of a dynamic culture to infuse the generation with a new hope and a revitalized inspiration for their homeland. Hence, Reines dreamed of a new methodology of Jewish culture. As we have already discussed, his plan for systematizing Halacha and Agadah into abstract concepts and essential principles of knowledge would give rise to the construction of a highly developed system of norms and regulations that would be governed by a logical order.

Reines was endowed with ceaseless energy. He traveled from one yeshiva to another—from Wolozin to Ishoshok. When he

---

[24] *Ibid.*, p. 5-11.

was fifteen he had begun to amass one scholarly paper after another, piling up his original ideas on the Talmud with notes and commentary of a massive and prodigious nature. As we are told by Maimon, when Reines was sixteen years of age, he was encouraged to explore mathematics and the famous work of the Rambam's, *Milas Ha-hegyon*. This was destined to make a very profound impression upon the mind of this budding young prodigy. Some years later he wrote three works which are still in manuscript form: *Rashit Bikurim*,[25] on codes; *Shoel Umashiv*,[26] a work on responsa of practical problems; and *Shusa Binuka*,[27] a compilation of notes on the Talmud.

"Zachor Zos L'Yaakov,"[28] is a biographical introduction by Rabbi Maimon Fishman which portrays the majestic personality of Reines. And who was Reines?—A man who was endowed with the unrelenting capacity to fulfill the mission that he had set out to accomplish. Reines frequently remarked that the masses tend to confuse and misconstrue many classical traditions that are encompassed in the Talmud. For example, let us examine the classic view concerning the thirty-six secret sages who uphold the world with their righteousness. These are not secret men, Reines exclaims, but rather are men who are courageous and dedicated in fulfilling and executing their ideas and principles however disparaging and humiliating they may appear in the eyes of the public. Reines was such a man who persevered and overcame all the obstacles and abuse that were heaped upon him by the various classes of Jewish notables. Reines is characterized as the *Zaddik Nistor*, who is willing to risk his fame and fortune, to sacrifice his total being for the ultimate commitment of his ideals.

One of Reines' great goals was to establish a new method of study within the framework of Talmudic logic. His *opus magnum* concerning this goal was crystallized in *Chosem Tochnis*,[29] a book containing the Halacha derivations from biblical pas-

---

[25] A discussion of this may be found in the introduction to I. J. Reines, *Noad Shel Dimos* (Jerusalem: Solomon, 1934).
[26] *Ibid.*
[27] *Ibid.*
[28] *Ibid.*
[29] Isaac Jacob Reines, *Shnei Hamoros*, pp.

sages and logical constructions from concepts and principles. This work created such fury in rabbinical and scholarly circles that it captured the fancy of none other than Rabbi Bezalel Vilner. Rabbi Bezalel Vilner expressed his great appreciation for this new contribution to the field of Talmudic scholarship. The work was hailed as a classic among the circles of the Haskalah men of that age. Articles were written about Reines' new advancements in the field of Talmudic scholarship in numerous languages; Russian, French, Hebrew and even Arabic.

We know that he was in close communication with Rabbi Zvi Hirsh Kalisher. Kalisher admired the young Rabbi Reines and acknowledged Reines' fortitude and zeal concerning this controversial issue. He was enthusiastic about this young rabbi who had not as yet established for himself a firm and secure social position among the rabbinical elite yet took the initiative to advance his original views relating to this vital issue.

Among the notables at the 1882 rabbinical convention at St. Petersburg were such notables as Joseph Baer Solovcitchik, Isaac Elchanan Spector and Eliahu Chaim Meisels of Lodz. There also appeared on the scene a young rabbi by the name of Reines. He agitated to advance a new program within the daily program of study for every student throughout all the yeshivas. His proposal was simply this—that Jewish students should be equipped with the knowledge of Russian and a general background of the principle sciences. Reines saw in this program a remedy for those students who forsook the yeshiva to attend the gymnasium and other secular schools. Thus the introduction of these studies would avert the threat and danger of the young Jewish student who was rapidly assimilating the cultural milieu of the secular environment. However, the older rabbinic leaders ignored Reines' plea and were content to maintain the status quo, namely, a continued program of complete isolation from all secular influences which may deter the student from his religious studies.

Reines did not lose faith in his convictions. He was convinced of the necessity of beginning a new venture, that of constructing a model yeshiva which made its first appearance in Shvinzin in the early 1880's. This plan had emerged too soon and he was confronted with many opponents who sought to undermine this new establishment. His adversaries to whom he referred in his *Shnei Hamoros*[30] were not zealous to uphold the law of G-d but were rather diligently eager to destroy this sincere attempt to establish a modern type yeshiva.

In 1883 Reines was taken prisoner by the Russian government because of his alleged subversive activities, and cast into prison for two days. The plan for establishing his model type yeshiva was foiled. His plan for a renaissance of yeshiva life did not come to fruition until several decades later. Before he was to accept his position at Lida he had received offers from many distant communities. From America and even from Manchester, England the call was sent out to seek Reines, for they had heard about his majestic personality and gifted attributes as a spiritual leader who could also meet the needs of the intellectual Jew. However he was reluctant to leave the center of Torah which was his native birthplace—Russia. He, therefore, declined these invitations and in the winter of 1884 assumed the pulpit in Lida. There he was destined to demonstrate his capability for leadership in the Jewish community.

In 1887, according to Maimon, Reines had confronted Rabbi Samuel Mohliver with a plan for rejuvenating the Jewish settlement in Israel. However extraordinary the plan seemed to Mohliver, he was reluctant to agree with Reines and he considered it fantastic. In his eyes the plan of nurturing a community in Israel with an economic and spiritual development was irrational and unreasonable at this time. Reines, however, did not desist from his original aspirations. Between the years that preceded the Mizrachi movement and his meeting with Mohliver, Reines engaged in a polemic to uphold and maintain the principles of resettling the Jews in Israel. His essay, *Netzach Yisroel*[31] published by his son, Moshe, and reprinted in Sinai 1937 is an incisive and critical statement concerning the issues involved with the development of a Jewish state. In that essay

---

[30] *Ibid.*

[31] Isaac Jacob Reines, "Netzach Yisroel," *Sinai*, Vol. III, R. Werfel, editor (Jerusalem: Mosad Ha Rav Kook, 1937), pp. 348-368.

he defends admirably his position to associate even with those who are transgressing the law and who are considered evil in the eyes of many orthodox Jews. This allegation, contended Reines, is mere hypocrisy and seeks to dissuade the average person from the true course and real issues that are to be examined. Briefly stated here we can express the main contention of Reines was to refute this false accusation. He premised his remarks on the foundation that there are two categories of mitzvoth—namely, between man and G-d, and between man and his fellow man. The orthodox or religious Jew is convinced that all the laws of the Torah are divinely instructed and guided by G-d. Laws of *tzitzoth* and *tefillin* are equally observed with those of *tzedakah* and *hashavoth avaydoh*. Traditional and rational mitzvoth both emanate from G-d and compliance of the mitzvoh is an expression of obedience to G-d's authority. There are certain groups within the Jewish community who although not adhering to the traditional precepts are nevertheless concerned and involved with the social mitzvoths. They abide by the social law from a rational and emotional response to enhance the safe-keeping and well-being of their brethren in the Diaspora. The only distinction between the orthodox and the non-observant Jews lies in the fact that the former views his obedience to the law from a totally religious aspect while the latter obeys the laws of communal welfare from a rational and emotional frame of reference. They are both seeking the same goals even though their method of attaining them or adhering to them is distinct in their conceptual approach to their performance. Now we see them in our own communities within the Diaspora and are associating with them on the social level. These so-called *chofshim* are completely involved and totally dedicated to the amelioration of the plight of their brethren in need of their monetary assistance. Not one will deride the performance of these mitzvohs even though the freethinkers are also participating in aiding their brethren. No one will claim that he should abdicate his concern for his brethren simply because the irreligious are also involved in the activity of helping the needy. Thus even if the irreligious cooperate in assisting the poor we should not relieve ourselves from complying and observing the vital mitzvoh of assuring the security of our people. Hence the mitzvoh of resettling Israel should be viewed within the same context. The resettling of Israel is beneficial not only for the individual but also for the entire Jewish community. The Torah states that you shall lend money to my nation. How can one truly observe this precept? Lending money to an entire nation is well-nigh impossible. However, if one assists and supports the Jewish state he has accomplished this task.[32]

Reines revealed the following about himself concerning his affiliation with the new movement of Zionism. He stood aside as a spectator to observe and examine to determine whether he should associate with the new organization. "This is my method," he contended, "To weigh all the factors concerning a given situation. There are *gedolim* who rush into a situation and invariably will become dispassionate and disconcerned with that particular situation. It is not so with me. I have always made it a point to examine all the factors that require one's attention to guide him along a course of action. Now I have looked upon the movement for two years and I have also explored the capabilities of the leader of this movement. Only then did I decide to participate in the organization with all its meetings and congresses."[33] There were many *gedolim* who attempted to dissuade Reines from associating and taking a deep interest in the movement. The renowned Chofetz Chaim went to him and pleaded with him for two hours. At first the Chofetz Chaim attempted to reason with him on a logical basis. Then he tried to persuade Reines on a personal level, that if he would remove his seal of approval from the movement then the Jewish world as it were would acknowledge Reines as a supreme leader in all areas that require the authority of Jewish leadership. Reines retorted that he must remain stubborn and retain his contention to support and uphold his opinions concerning Zionism. Furthermore, he added that there are many rabbis who would also associate and ally themselves with the new move-

---

[32] Fishman, *op. cit.*, p. 8.
[33] *Ibid.*, p. 12.

ment. However, they fear the social pressures of the older *gedolim* and therefore, are contented with maintaining the status quo.

Reines in defending the rise of Zionism declared that freethinkers do not depreciate the value of rebuilding the state of Israel. Moreover, it is a tribute to the new cause to observe how those who are removed from the spiritual ideas that govern the ethical attitudes and moral beliefs are nevertheless deeply concerned and totally committed to the exalted goal of securing and assuring the welfare and safekeeping of the Jewish people. Reines actually participated in all its congresses and in 1902 prepared the groundwork for a systematic reconstruction of a religious wing within the total framework of the Zionist organization.

Reines, as we know, had many opponents within the religious circle who condemned and criticized him vehemently. Here is an incident that characterizes the abuse that was heaped upon him. When Reines was in Kovno for a speaking engagement he arrived there on Friday. That Shabbos he spent with Rabbi Zvi Rabinowitz discussing with the latter various problems in Halacha and the Jewish situation at large. On Saturday night a great number of Jews had assembled in the synagogue to hear Reines deliver a discourse on the involvement in the new religious movement, Mizrachi. The synagogue was packed and among the listeners was an ultra-pious man who with great emotion snatched Reines' coat and tore it. Everyone present became enraged at this act and Reines had all he could do to prevent the crowd from assaulting the fanatic.[34]

Max Nordau had a deep sense of appreciation for Reines and lauded him for his patience, scholarship, wisdom and optimism in the ultimate hope of Jewish redemption. Reines retained his religiosity and did not sway to the position for the enlightened men of the Zionist movement. He was fond of making this remark: The enlightened Zionist say that he who is not a Zionist is not to be considered even as a Jew but I say that any Zionist who is not a Jew in the true sense is not really

---

[34] *Ibid.*, p. 15.

a Zionist. Although he was passionately involved in the advancement of the movement he was always concerned with maintaining the religious identity of the orthodox wing. Once a religious Jew was filled with anger because Reines wanted to establish a separate federation within the Zionist movement, namely Mizrachi. That religious Jew contended that we are all aware of the Midrashic passage concerning the four minim that we take on the Succoth holiday. The four minim symbolize the various degrees of religious commitment with Judaism. "All must be taken together," exclaimed the Polish Jew, "So how can you, Reines, embark upon a plan to establish a separate group. Let us all fuse into one unit so that we may avoid dissension and discord within the entire organization. Reines calmly answered and refuted the excitable person. The esrog is never taken in the same binding as the other three minim. The esrog stands alone for it aims to symbolize its specific value in contrast to the others. The esrog denotes the perfect religious Jew. Thus even though the four minim are taken together, yet at times the religious Jew must preserve his ideals and maintain his separateness as we observe with regard to the esrog.[35]

Even Nahum Sokolow marveled at the exuberant delivery and energetic emotional speeches that Reines conveyed at the various Zionist congresses. The yeshiva that Reines established at Lida, as we have previously mentioned, was called Torah V'Daath, a harmony between Torah and general knowledge. Reines in a letter addressed to Fishman communicated his emotional feelings that he too would like to settle in the land for which he exhausted all his energy and strived to rebuild—the homeland of our nation with the restoration of its original glory. However, as we know World War I had broken out, communication was interrupted and soon after Reines died. He never attained the fruition of successfully experiencing his lifelong dreams which he unceasingly aspired to achieve.

Reines attested to his own astuteness in being able to master countless folio in his literary creativity. He declared that in his youth he had made a covenant to produce every day original ideas and novel concepts navigating the intrepid waters in the

---

[35] *Ibid.*, p. 18.

vast sea of the Talmud. He depicted himself as a man with a gravitating emotional stress immersed in the traumatic problems and the turbulent perplexities that confronted his age and challenged his environment.

History, contended Reines, depends upon *regesh*. The disintegration of society becomes evident only when there is an abandonment of hope and the disastrous feeling of complete despair. His optimism and faith in the continuity of the unique mission confirmed in the historical covenant between Israel and G-d provided him with the inspiration to write with a prolific pen. The idea of transmitting culture to future generations presents one with an exalted task to write his ideas and record them as an everlasting memorial.[36]

One characteristic essential to the spiritual development of Reines was his desire to communicate to others and to inculcate them with the majestic beauty and intellectual creativity that is inherent within the entire scope of Jewish literature. He who teaches others Torah is one who is endowed with a higher degree of spiritual perfection and should not be satisfied if he alone can be gratified. However, he must always endeavor to influence others in becoming closer in cleaving unto G-d. The medieval writers expressed this by stating that if one would have ascended to heaven to see the entire galaxy of the universe on his return he would be compelled to express his opinions and diffuse his knowledge to others. As the prophet Jeremiah had thought: I will no longer mention nor speak in G-d's name. Then, however, he could not retain his position of stillness and quietude—rather he must express and convey the work of G-d for it was like a fire consuming his bones and he could not refrain any longer from announcing his prophecy. The same angel who is appointed to declare the growth, maturation and development of every blade of grass is the one who is sent to infuse and kindle within man the spark of expression and he tells man: Reveal and disclose all what you have studied. The method of man's genius for expression is a two-fold process. Speaking and lecturing and all other forms of personal delivery

---

[36] Isaac Jacob Reines, *Sharay Orah*, (Vilna: Rom, 1886), p. 7.

are essential in communicating the spiritual message by the person who is endowed with a desire to contribute his knowledge and experience to others. When G-d infused within man the divine spirit the commentaries denote that it was the ability of man to speak and to communicate his ideas to his neighbors. However, speaking before a public audience or delivering a lecture has an inherent limitation for one can only reach a minute audience and only those who are in close proximity to the lecturer can benefit from it. There is another more inclusive manner of diffusing one's ideas and conveying one's thoughts to a public far greater than his immediate audience. This is through the method of writing and publishing. All forms of writing whether it is a letter, article or book, reach the reader wherever he may reside. Therefore, the man who is interseted in making his knowledge known to all persons should be equipped with the skills of writing. Hence writing is the necessary tool that is indispensable if one is to communicate on a broader universal scale his ideas to any public. Writing, moreover, is the essence of exploring the definitive nature and essential quality with which the writer is endowed. Now the Midrash expresses the idea that Israel is likened unto a bird. As a bird needs wings to fly so must Israel write and publish in order to express and communicate her ideas. The rabbis commented in Shabbos on the phrase *anochi*—I am, G-d, your G-d. What is the meaning of *anochi* they asked? I, alone, says G-d, have written this law and given it to you. The writing of the Torah therefore is the intrinsic quality that characterizes the communication of ideas and is the media of recording events from one generation to another.[37]

Reines was not only anxious to create in the halachic system of the Talmud a revolutionary and highly advanced conceptualized methodology. He was also eager to advance his original way of thinking to the homiletic midrashim and legendary passages of the Talmud.

In all of Reines' writings there is his stamp of singular orig-

---

[37] Isaac Jacob Reines, *Or Shivat Ha-Yomim:* Introduction, (Vilna: Rom, 1896), I, p. 8.

inality. His goal[38] and purpose was to infuse and ignite the spark and the glitter of Judaism to all his people with a burning love and animated desire to attain the ultimate ideal of complete spiritual devotion to G-d. His love for the spirit of Torah enraged him at times and with a fierce anger and a turbulent temper he denounced those who sought to make a mockery of the Talmud and who heaped words of abuse and disparagement against its sacred literature.

Reines in an address to the Zionist Organization in St. Petersburg decried the loud clamor of the radical right who sought to annul the efforts of the Zionist movement.[39] If they would have criticized with logical proofs the erroneous conception of the movement then we would have reasonable ground to disprove their false contentions. Now, however, all they can express in their loud cries are protests filled with malicious propaganda and countless snide remarks that only echo the empty reasoning of their arguments. We can only express a sigh of exhaustion or weep with bitter tears because of the animosity of our brethren which is ill-founded and baseless. In all the Diaspora there is oppression, discrimination and unbearable torment which has gripped the pulse of our people. The Jewish community is engulfed in a sea of terror, in an ocean of distress. Our sons and daughters are being lured and deduced by the secular culture and its environment. The level of education has sunk almost to the abyss. Our schools, classrooms and teachings are abating, decreasing with a stifling rapidity. Our hope and unity that has characterized the Jewish people for so many centuries has been transformed into disillusion and discord. Truly everyone can observe the obvious rate of disintegration that has confronted the pride of our people. And now in the midst of all this stress and strife there appeared on the scene as though an angel sent from heaven—the advent of the new Zionist idea —to resurrect our people and to revive the Jewish community. This has given new direction and new course to guide our people to assume once again the invigorated hope and national

---

[38] Isaac Jacob Reines, *Eduth B'Yaacov*—Sermon II, (Vilna: Dvorzetz, 1872), p. 17.
[39] Isaac Jacob Reines, *Noad Shel Dimos*, p. 18.

pride that is essential for survival. It has stemmed the tide of assimilation and has brought a fresh approach to all aspects of Jewish activity. All this, the Zionist idea which calls for the establishment of a refuge and a haven for our people, many of our brethren continue to malign and pursue with zeal and fervor the undermining and destruction of the forward progress of the movement. And why do they proceed with this course of action? They are all personal reasons of self-glorification and self-aggrandizement. The *charadim* should accept the Zionist people with open arms. The orthodox should aim to restore them to higher religious goals and not to persecute them for their non-observance of the religious code. The idea that the Zionists are intent upon maintaining the pride of our nation should be reason enough to try to inculcate them with the love of G-d and His precepts.[40]

Rabbi J. J. Weinberg depicted the extraordinary personality of Reines and his indelible imprint upon the Zionist movement. When we speak of Reines we cannot define him in particular terms but we must incorporate within a broad context his universal influence. Everyone is familiar and well-acquainted with his almost superhuman achievements both in leadership and scholarship. When we talk about Reines we discuss the logic of Reines, the *drush* of Reines, the Mizrachi of Reines and the Yeshiva of Reines. All these are his accomplishments and therefore his role in 20th century Jewry is one of magnificent magnitude and electrifying scope. Everyone who experienced his presence was astonished and overwhelmed at the unusual and unique qualities which were inherent in Reines. Within him was a phenomenal understanding of the old traditional Talmudic text harmonized with a fresh and vibrant approach concerning the task towards surmounting the immediate perilous problems that were confronting and challenging the very roots and foundations of Judaism. At the St. Petersburg convention Reines chose to express his personal convictions concerning the introduction of some secular studies within the curriculum of the yeshivas and he was destined to live in isolation.[41]

---

[40] *Ibid.*, p. 11.
[41] *Ibid.*, p. 12.

At the turn of the 20th century many young rabbis were engulfed in dilemma. They knew and felt that some change in the religious order of the Jewish community was imperative. However, they were extremely reluctant to forsake the position of rigid conformity that was advocated by the older rabbis. Reines was acknowledged as an older rabbi of notable fame who had transferred to the camp of the younger rabbis. He mantled the garb of energetic youth and was a symbol of progressive action that would inspire the young rabbis who were looking for leadership and seeking the advice and support of an older rabbi.

It is quite interesting to learn of Reines' position concerning the Uganda question. It is a well-known fact that Reines was one of those who supported the original Herzl plan of acquiring a territory other than Israel to establish a state as a refuge for afflicted and oppressed Jews. Reines never contemplated that Uganda was a final course of action towards resolving the problem of saving the Jewish people. He rather sought a compromise between the Zionists and the Territorialists. He writes in glowing terms of Zangwill concerning the acquisition of some territory that would assure the security and well-being of many unfortunate and neglected Jews. However important and expedient this plan of territorial acquisition per se would be nevertheless Reines could not agree with it in its entirety. This should only be a temporary and intermediate stage to achieve and attain the higher goal of the resettling of Israel. No true Zionist can be contented if he were to discontinue his hopes concerning the realization of a rejuvenated homeland in Israel. The Zionist movement has come about to resolve the national question and to seek a positive program towards the issue of national redemption. However, a final conclusion can be reached only if the Jews return to their fatherland. Moreover, the land of Israel is the causal nexus for historic destiny and it is the intrinsic source of pride that has kept alive Jewish national aspirations for salvation. There, The International Territorialist Organization, can only serve as a transition point to lead the way for aspiring and achieving the successful goal of resettling Israel.[42]

At 60 years Reines assumed the helm of leadership in the organization that he had so arduously and admirably fought for and championed. At that time his physical condition was extremely debilitated. Suffering from gallstones he was still stalwart enough in spirit to wage a courageous battle of raising the banner of Judaism.

We have seen from the various articles that have been presented, the two-fold qualities inherent within the dynamic personality of Reines. His gifted attributes in the field of Jewish leadership and his indelible imprint on future Jewry was discussed and analyzed. We have also attempted to depict Reines as the ingenious Rosh Yeshiva, dean of the Lida Academy, and forerunner of the advent of a new model yeshiva that would encompass a dual program to guide the student. Reines, therefore, has placed himself in the book of everlasting Jewish historical memory. With his burning animated spirit and unique logical mind he has harmonized within himself a singular position in 20th century Jewry. He is remembered and revered as both a Rosh Yeshiva and *manhig yisroel,* teacher and leader.

---

[42] *Ibid.*

# 2

# Views on Man's Spiritual Development

## THE NATURAL AND THE SUPERNATURAL

Nature is the subject matter of G-d. All natural phenomena are considered to be experienced as miracles. The daily routines, however, in man's life becloud the concept that every natural act is of a miraculous nature.[1] The light of G-d is encased in nature. Hence nature is only the external shell that reflects the internal illumination of G-d.[2] Nature, contends Reines, is the candelabra of G-d. Within it burns the light of G-d. The supernatural and the natural mirror man's behavior toward G-d. If man reacts in a supreme manner, G-d will respond to him in an extraordinary way. However, if man acts according to his natural instincts then G-d will only accord him ordinary supervision.[3]

Concerning the blessing that one gives if he is saved from peril *Birchat Hagomel*, Reines interprets the following: The Talmud relates that if one is saved from danger he must recite the blessing of *Hagomel* before 10 people. Two of them should be scholars. The question is why does this personal blessing require a quorum of 10 including among them at least two scholars? Reines offers the suggestion that the blessing of *Hago-*

---
[1] Isaac Jacob Reines, *Sharay Orah*, p. 13.
[2] Isaac Jacob Reines, *Or Shivat Ha-Yomim*, II, p. 31.
[3] Isaac Jacob Reines, *Sefer Harochim*, p. 195.

*mel* is the supreme test of man to realize that within the scope of natural events and occurrences G-d has delivered him and rescued him from peril. We know that for many miracles, a person need not recite the blessing of *Hagomel*—all that is required is to give thanks for redemption. The blessing of *Hagomel* however, is indicative of the realization of G-d's grace although it is not self-revealing. Therefore the requirement of scholars and a public audience is to attest that he has truly discerned G-d's intervention on his behalf.[4]

Defining natural and supernatural occurrences, Reines suggests that nature is a slow and gradual process while the supernatural is immediate and striking. Hence the realization of G-d through nature is more intricate and hidden while the realization of G-d through a wonderous act is revealing to all.[5] *Nes* that we have interpreted thus far to mean as the supernatural intervention of G-d is also the expression symbolizing the flag. That is to say, just as the flag is seen by the multitudes, likewise is the miracle recognized by many. Another meaning for the *Nes* is remembrance. Rashi interprets the phrase in *Deuteronomy* 26, *V'haya L'cha L'Nes*, to mean as a remembrance. Hence the object of the *Nes* is that its influence is compelling and dramatic to the masses at large. Contrasting therein the term *teva* means something which is engraved. The natural way of G-d's supervision in life is hidden and we do not see any magnificent wonders of His glory. As the word *matbea*, the picture on the coin is engraved within the copper, equally so is G-d's way mysteriously blurred within the routine of nature. The terms *nes* and *teva* not only have an intellectual distinction in view but their contrast can be discerned within the philological context of their meaning.[6]

The religious experience of man's quest for G-d is personified by observing the order within nature. We are reminded in Sanhedrin 44 of the dictum of Rabbi Jehudah that he who blesses the new moon receives the reward as though he were accepting the Divine Presence. The word analogy between

---

[4] *Ibid.*
[5] *Ibid.*, p. 123.
[6] Isaac Jacob Reines, *Orah V'Simchah* (Vilna: Rom. 1899), p. 184.

*hachodesh hazeh lochem* and *zeh Eli v'anvehu* designates the aforementioned idea. The realization of the Divine Presence is perceived through the natural geophysical phenomenon. Thus the blessings of the new moon are the realization of G-d through nature.[7]

The nature of a person is to succeed in a gradual status or otherwise he deteriorates slowly. Sudden affluence or extreme depression to be sure does not satisfy man for he likes to experience his own creative ability. Man also cannot withstand a sudden breakdown of all his material splendor and glorious creative workmanship. The nature of man therefore is to benefit gradually and to retire slowly.[8]

The natural and supernatural occurrences in the world are the manifestations of G-d's relationship to the world and to humanity. How then does man react towards G-d? What is the media of man's expression for his religious commitment to G-d? This we shall comprehend when we begin to discuss the concept of *regesh*.

Reines contends that the emotional response of man towards G-d is a primary force in our creative Halachah. It is a known principle that for the purpose of saving human life all the laws of the Torah are discarded and we are commanded to transgress them except for three sins, namely; idolatry, adultery and murder.

Concerning the importance of human life it was also remarked by Rabbi Akiba and Rabbi Tarphon that if we were to be in a Sanhedrin not a single man would be put to death for any crime at any time. Now then we come to a problem for we find in the Talmud Sanhedrin 81 the declaration of the Mishnah that if one steals a vessel from the Sanctuary, etc., then zealots are permitted to slay him. The Gemorah comments on this that if the zealots would come to the court to ask a question whether it is permitted to slay such a transgressor, the court would be forbidden to issue an order of execution. However, the zealot may kill only a violator of the law if he is in hot pursuit of the criminal. The apparent anomaly is obvious, for

---

[7] Isaac Jacob Reines, *Shnei Hamoros*, I, p. 18.
[8] *Ibid.*, p. 19.

at first glance we are confronted with the almost invincibility of the preservation of human life while equally we observe how a person for the sake of the law can be a self-appointed prosecutor. Reines proceeds to give the rationale for this apparent paradox. In time of *regesh* when a Jew is confronted with the fact that his co-religionist has committed an atrocity he may proceed under certain circumstances as prescribed in the Mishnah Sanhedrin 81 to eradicate the man who has committed the criminal offense. *Kanaim pogim bo* is the test of the zealot's supreme emotional feeling that he cannot and must not ignore and neglect the word of G-d. Hence only in the time when the abhorrent act is being committed can the zealot proceed to act on his own accord. The Torah has issued the privilege to the zealot only in the precise moment when the precept of the law is being violated. At that instant the zealot is allowed to slay the transgressor for then the Torah recognizes his act of *regesh* as true and noble.

The quality of *regesh* that is to awaken within man the spirit to attain closeness to G-d may come gradually and through the routine functioning of ritual. Reines proceeds to explain why the Rabbis felt that even if one is not involved in the study of Torah for its true purpose *shelo lishma* nevertheless the act of study per se shall lead and guide him to the real purpose of Torah study. Reines attempts to explain this as comparable to one's routine activities in his physical cleanliness. When a person who is not an esthete washes and bathes himself constantly then he will realize that this is an important function for his physical well-being. This routine will motivate him to become involved in taking proper care necessary to secure his daily cleanliness. The result of spiritual study and spiritual obligations to G-d is essentially the same. The normal operation and habitual obedience to the Torah and to its study will cause man to become emotionally involved and spiritually motivated to the true purpose and the higher goal of the Torah, namely the *lishma* of it.

### FUNCTIONAL MITZVOHS AND EMOTIONAL MITZVOHS

Just as the medieval Jewish philosophers sought to make a a polarity of reasoning and explanation for the mitzvohs, namely, Saadiah's *shmiot sichliot*, Reines was likely concerned to present his interpretation of the mitzvohs. His system of catoregization is practical and emotive mitzvohs *maasiot v'regeshiot*.

The practical mitzvohs can also be accomplished with *regesh*. However the essential purpose is the fulfillment of the act, for example—*lulab*. There is a group of mitzvohs whose quality is intrinsically one of spirit and emotional dedication, namely, *ahavta adonai* and *ahavta yisroel*—love of G-d and Israel.

Just as functional mitzvohs are essentially apart from emotional mitzvohs, similarly there are rational mitzvohs which are not intrinsically emotional in their nature and scope. Mitzvohs that are fulfilled from a rational point of view however may contain the qualities of emotion and spiritual fervor.[9]

We have explained that nature is gradual and slow while the supernatural is immediate and striking. Similarly this idea is prevalent within the concept of *regesh*. There is an emotional drive to a mitzvoh that is arrived at by a process of methodical and logical reasoning. There is also another means by which the person arrives at the mitzvoh with *regesh*. It is through a sudden and striking manner that grips the person who in turn becomes filled with an enthusiasm and ecstasy for the mitzvoh.[10] As we have defined the distinction between rational *regesh* and devotional *regesh* we can understand the expressed desire on behalf of those who are completely devoid of theological orthodox Judaism to be deeply concerned with the problems that engulf the Jewish community. The free thinkers although not observing and participating in the theocracy of the Jewish community are however moved by a moral obligation to be dedicated to their brethren. We see in our own times that many communal projects and care for the needy are supported in a great measure by those who do not observe practical mitzvohs. Their *regesh*, their desire and devotion, although not imbued with the traditional sense of emotional passion, is however inspired with a rational desire and dedication to the Jewish national cause.

---

[9] Isaac Jacob Reines, *Sefer Harochim*, p. 9.
[10] Isaac Jacob Reines, *Or Chodosh Al Zion*, p. 53.

Therefore, we should not appraise lightly their sincerity to advance and to improve the communal life of the Jewish people.[11]

There is at times a *regesh* which is devoid of any intellectual and critical meaning. It is built upon fantasy and imagination and lack of concise thought. This is precisely the reason why the Rabbis allowed the nullification of vows. The Rabbis were well aware of the fact that man is gripped with senseless emotion. This futile emotion creates a drive and passion that often misdirects and misguides man. Logic becomes displaced with emotional acts that will inevitably lead the man who makes the rational vows to regret his previous pledge. Therefore the concept of *hatoras nedarim* demonstrates that the Rabbis were aware of man's psychic drives and irrational behavior. The elasticity of nullifying a vow is a safety valve that controls man's emotions within the sphere of Halachah. Reines interprets this to mean *regesh*. The emotion, passion and the whole psychic structure of man is the chain that binds man to a certain course of action. Man is led almost blindly by the passion that motivates his direction. Therefore, *regesh* is the factor upon which the delicate structure of the human being is developed and perfected.[12]

The degree of one's fulfillment of the mitzvohs can be measured in various levels of dedication. There are those who perform the mitzvoh as a mechanical response to the social environment surrounding them *mitzvah anashim melvmada*. Yet another group accepts the responsibility of a mitzvoh solely because it is G-d's command for man to execute the mitzvoh according to the law prescribed in the Torah. Another group experiences great emotion when they fulfill the obligations of the Torah. Their response to the mitzvoh is one of inspiration and dedication. The mitzvoh gives them the zeal to go forward and to experience the idea of G-d. Finally, there are men who have already experienced sufficient devotion and dedication to G-d which enables them to be men of piety and of great virtue.

---

[11] R. Werfel, "Netzach Israel-Mamor Chibat Zion," *Sinai*, III (1937), p. 358.

[12] Isaac Jacob Reines, *Shei Hamoros*, p. 42.

Nevertheless, they are not comforted by the mere experience of emotional response. The mitzvoh not only warrants the act of aspiring with emotion to G-d, fulfilling their own personal needs but also executing the obligation above and beyond the psychological necessity of their emotional need for religious expression.[13]

Concerning the aforementioned division of categories within the concept of *regesh*, we understand the problem posed in the Talmud. What is greater—a man who observes the mitzvohs even though he personally is not duty bound to abide by them or the one who observes the mitzvohs because he is compelled by their laws and held responsible for their observance. The theory behind this problem is the following: can *regesh* alone be sufficient as far as man's obedience to G-d or is there another element that is necessary, namely, the complete subservience to G-d above one's own personal feeling.

It would appear to be resolved in the Gemorah that *gadol hamitzuvoh mami sheeno mitzuvoh*. Greater is he who is required by law to observe than the one who complies to the will of G-d from his own volition. Emotional response may not always be prevalent hence a man who is under supreme tension will evade the law, thereby seeking to rationalize and thereby not always responding to the duty of the law. Therefore, man must have a super-compelling force, namely, the divine order of the Torah to guide and direct him through all times however painstaking it may be to observe and maintain the mitzvoh.

The emotional stimulus for our homeland is an important phenomenon to assure Jewish survival. He who is emotionally tied to the land of Israel will himself become spiritually elevated. In contrast, the person who is devoid of feeling for his homeland degrades his own spiritual personality. The one who has an historical identity and is filled with passion for his homeland will be inspired to be a more religious person for he will remember with nostalgia and longing the pride of his heritage. Just as a person who inherits money or property from his deceased relative is gladdened how much more, then, should he

---

[13] Isaac Jacob Reines, *Sharay Orah*, p. 57.

enjoy it and become enriched from the great heritage of our forefathers—the promised land of Israel.[14]

When one is engaged in a battle he will be victorious only if he is imbued with a high degree of morale. He must be impressed with either his physical prowess or strategical know-how or to be under such pressure that the value that this war will produce is indeed worth risking his entire life for what he has already gained. Similarly is the battle for spiritual devotion to G-d. A man must be imbued with the idea that life is a battle against the evil forces that tend to mislead and misguide one from the path of G-dliness.[15]

World history is replete with many tales about generals or kings who were stricken with illness or disease and who rose to the supreme test of withstanding their own personal tragedies to accomplish the task of warfare successfully. After the war was completed however, their spirit evaporated. Once again they were engulfed in their personal problems no longer able to rise.[16]

The battlefield deserves complete physical stamina yet all soldiers are accompanied by martial music—songs of victory for the defeat of the enemy. This is to instill courage and inspire the soldiers on the battlefield. Thereby we observe that these songs are a key factor designed for emerging victorious in battle. Man's physical well-being must entail an intrinsic commitment a feeling of dedication to the goals of his battle. Hence the spiritualizing strategy of winning the battle of territorial gain can be transferred to the Jewish historical quest for national identity. It must encompass a vigorous outpour of our emotional expression to G-d.

Interestingly enough the Talmud relates that if someone has talked during the laying of tefillin between his hand and his head it is considered a transgression so flagrant as to warrant his dismissal from the battlefield. The question is what is meant by that metaphorical expression in the Talmud? Reines suggests that the tefillin of the hand and the head represents a unity

---

[14] Isaac Jacob Reines, *Or Chodosh Al Zion*, p. 40.
[15] *Ibid.*, p. 62.
[16] *Ibid.*, p. 64.

between man's thought and action, the theoretical and the practical, the ideal and the real. If one talks between the ceremony of placing the tefillin on himself it is evident that he lacks the continuity of thought and action. The tefillin is the historical bridge of the gap which lies between man's thought and action.

The spirit of martyrdom that is historic within Jewish tradition has been advanced and championed at first by individual leaders, men who were endowed with an iron-clad will for the dedication and devotion to G-d and His Torah. Rabbi Jehudah Ben Baba is a celebrated figure of this type who was able to make the supreme test of his own personal self-sacrifice for G-d. He alone will be remembered for good. Without him, the Gemorah proceeds to relate, the laws of *Knasot* would have been abandoned in Israel: He had the courage and fortitude to ordain five students, namely, Rabbi Meir, Rabbi Shimon, Rabbi Yehudah, Rabbi Yosi and Rabbi Nechemyah while under the piercing fire of the Roman arrows. He was endowed with the spirit that looks forward insensitive to the needs of his own body. The sense of devotion to G-d is created from the spirit of mind sublimating one's passions for his temporal physical needs by timeless goals and a desire to reach the ultimate ideal of purity and piety.[17]

The sin of the *meraglim* as explained by Reines came about through a void and lack of *regesh*. It was a complete and utter feeling of surrender to the great powers of the Canaanites and other nations. "They are strong and mighty—how can we conquer them. They are insurmountable—how can we overcome them?" These statements are a result of an insensitivity to man's total dedication and complete spiritual devotion to the promised land of Israel. The lack of spiritual fervor for the land of Israel was the essential factor that brought about the catastrophe for the *dor hamidbar*.[18]

There are two intrinsic forms of *regesh* that form the Jewish soul—the spirit for his religion and the spirit for his nationality.[19] There is theoretical *regesh* and practical *regesh* or latent

---

[17] Isaac Jacob Reines, *Orah Visimchah*, p. 31.
[18] Isaac Jacob Reines, *Or Chodosh Al Zion*, p. 172.
[19] Isaac Jacob Reines, *Orah V'Simchah*, p. 8.

*regesh* and when the appropriate time arises, the time that begs of him to give for his religion and people, this latent spirit assumes a manifest and declared spirit of dedication *b'poel* and *b'koach*.[20]

There is also another duality within the concept of *regesh*—internal *regesh* and external *regesh*. The former is derived from a sincere movement of the spirit, a dynamic involvement in the religious participation in observance of the mitzvoh. However the reverse type of this principle is the external feeling that moves the person to become involved spiritually. Hence the dual function of *ahavas* and *yiras adonai* is the very essence of this duality. Love is internal devotion while fear is manifested by external forces created by the environment. Love is natural and internal; fear is artificial and external. We can, therefore, understand why the Ramban chose to explain why a positive precept overrides a negative precept. *Asey doche losaseh*.

The phrase in the proverb that through his life he shall appear to be irrational demonstrates the idea that he who is filled with *regesh* will appear strange in the eyes of he who is lacking it.[21]

"The fire of Torah," proclaims the Midrash in Koheleth Rabbah, "has been everlasting for me." That is to say, the Torah that one learns with extreme fervor and complete spiritual devotion is the guide for a Torah-existing life.[22] If one does not have any spiritual devotion, if one is devoid of a feeling of commitment for the precepts of the Torah, how may he recognize his spiritual malady? Are there any signs whereby one can discern his spiritual deterioration? There are however certain symptoms according to Reines. If one loses his self-respect and has no feeling of personal dignity and ethical steadfastness he is indefinitely devoid of the proper attitude for the service of G-d. However, a lack of appearing to be glorious and also the feeling of being downtrodden and humiliated does not at all times mean that the person is failing in his service to G-d. There is at times a temporary void in one's feeling of dignity. This

---

[20] *Ibid.*, p. 10.
[21] *Ibid.*, p. 13.
[22] *Ibid.*, p. 14.

void is brought about in order to assume higher goals. Hence a person at times must sublimate his own glory and assume painstaking humility to ascend to a more glorious position in life.[23]

There are two kinds of nullification. Sometimes a thing ceases to be permanently while on the other hand it is only of a temporary nature. Just as in the course of human events there are two kinds of voidability, this dichotomy exists in the area of human development. If the drive for dignity has completely disappeared and once personal pride has been completely defeated there can be no longer a resurrection of spirit. However, if the lack of one's dignity and the feeling of his pride is superficial, it has only lost its external glamor but still retains its internal glow then there is hope for rejuvenation. Perhaps the entire problem of understanding the secret of Jewish survival can be explained in terms of only an external disappearance of its national dignity. Israel has never lost its internal self-sacrificing mission. Throughout all its persecutions and pogroms Jews have always awaited the Messianic Era of salvation and the cessation of the whole dark era that has beclouded us within the Diaspora. The feeling of *achris hayomim,* when the Messiah will come, is not just a fanciful phrase. It demonstrates the inner perseverance of the Jewish nation. It declares to the world with a clarion call that although Jews appear to be shattered Jews are easy prey for an aristocratic feeling of pride. Judaism is correlated with humanity. They both seek the ideal of man's dignity. It is a law that he who eats in the market place has forfeited his right for bearing testimony in a process of litigation. The reason being that he has degraded his own character hence we may assume that he may bear false testimony for the sake of some personal gain. A man who is not aware of his self-respect cannot elevate himself to the virtue of modesty. It is not merely one's own personal dignity that is required as an expression of emotional devotion to G-d rather it is also a feeling of national dignity that is warranted from the Jew. It is told in Midrashic literature that the splitting of

---

[23] Isaac Jacob Reines, *Or Chodosh Al Zion,* p. 50.

the sea came about by a deep sense of collective pride. The Bible is a bit ambiguous for it is written: And the Jews entered into the sea at the shore. The question is if they were in the sea how can they maintain their presence at the shore. The answer is that until the Jewish people took the daring step to dive into the sea no splitting had occurred. The Jewish people brought about the miracle of the splitting only because they were completely dedicated to the service of G-d. They had the opportunity either to sink in the sea or return to Egypt to assume the burden of servitude. They were confronted with two alternatives—slavery or annihilation. They chose the latter for cultural death is much more difficult than physical. Their salvation came about because they expressed a sincere desire to assume a new cultural identity. Natural pride therefore is an imperative for the existence of the Jewish community and moreover for serving G-d.[24]

National pride is a key element for the assurance of its survival. When the Canaanites heard that Aaron died, that also the clouds of glory that were guiding the Jews had ceased to operate, they declared war. The Canaanites felt that Aaron's demise was a result of a devaluation of Jewish pride brought about by their lack of commitment to G-d. Hence national survival is dependent upon national pride. The Canaanites thought that the Jewish national pride had suffered a terrific blow; therefore, they contended that the time was ripe to conquer and humiliate the Jewish people.

Patience is described as a true symbol of pride. To have the courage of controlling oneself is the supreme test of one's dignity. Patience manifests itself with the individual person and with the collective nation. Therefore, the Jewish people although they have been stripped of their external pride and glory nevertheless are keenly aware of their internal majestic beauty. For this Jews pray in their high holy ritual: G-d give glory to your nation—the idea being that internal patience can become so difficult that Jews may not be able to withstand the overwhelming pressure of the brutal suffering that has been

---

[24] *Ibid.*, p. 52.

endured for so many centuries. We ask G-d for external glory—a pride that should be visible to all, a pride declaring to the world of nations that Jews are not an imaginary people. Although Jews have been stripped of their homeland they profess to remain a nation chosen unto G-d to fulfill His glory and to communicate His message to the world about them.

Maimonides explains that the positive mitzvoh incorporates love within its sphere of observance while the negative mitzvoh constitutes merely fear of G-d. According to Reines' explanation we can understand Maimonides' dichotomy of love and fear of G-d—*asey docheh lo saaseh*.[25]

Internal devotion prevents man from being routinized and apathetic towards his devotion to G-d. We know that the habitual activities of man tend to dissuade him from the passionate way of his observance of mitzvoth. Hence man must be constantly aware of the external forces of environmental pressures that are designed to make him static towards his observance of the mitzvoth. Then only his intellectual and internal awareness for G-d can preserve him when he confronts the vast problems of society.[26]

The emotion that one experiences from the sense of sight is deeper and more pervasive than the emotion one experiences from the sense of hearing. As the Lamentor depicted it: My eyes wail unto my soul more than all of those whom I have heard wailing in the cities about the destruction of my nation—the idea of being that the sense of my own personal witnessing of the destruction and ruins of Jerusalem has impressed upon my soul a feeling far greater and far more indelible than what I have heard tell about its decimation.[27]

There are two faces in mankind that make an impact upon his soul, namely, good and evil. Man is confronted with two approaches to life, the noble and the barbaric. According to tradition, if one abides by the law then he will become enriched with the abundance of the land. However, if he scorns G-d

---

[25] Isaac Jacob Reines, *Sefer Harochim*, p. 12.
[26] Isaac Jacob Reines, *Noad Shel Dimos* (Jerusalem: Solomon, 1934), p. 38.
[27] Isaac Jacob Reines, *Or Chodosh Al Zion*, p. 41.

then he will be consumed by the sword. The Rabbis comment on this verse: Two objects descended to the world below—the book and the sword. This is to denote the drive and will to lead a good life and the drive for the contrary. The Midrash continues: If man will abide by the law then this book will serve as a shield to guide and maintain him throughout the perilous course and historical travail of his destiny. Hence it is expected of the Jewish people that they accept the book, the laws and ethics of the Torah. The true way of life is the striving for what is written in the book rather than the abhorrent inclination for exercising the sword.[28]

Reines now compares spiritual *regesh* and material *regesh*. The concepts are interrelated for just as all physical life must be endowed with movement, dynamism, likewise must spiritual *regesh* be endowed with a certain spark of dynamism. Without movement, growth and development there cannot be life and material matter. Hence concerning spiritual life man must be inspired and have the capacity to ignite within himself the spirit for the devotion to G-d and His law. The spirit and the law are considered as a coal and flame that are interconnected.[29]

The wicked people even when they are alive are considered dead. The righteous even in death are considered alive. The Midrash continues to explain why the wicked are considered as dead—for they see the sun rise and set, yet they do not make the proper blessings: *Yotzer or maariv aravim*. The explanation behind this dictum is that the wicked are devoid of *regesh*, hence they lack the feeling of Godliness. The righteous bequeath to us the spirit and fervor for the devotion and dedication to G-d.[30]

To the house of G-d we shall walk with emotion. The house of G-d denoting the synagogue has always been for the Jewish people a citadel of inspiration. The synagogue has always been considered as a place of social gathering and a collective meeting house for the whole community. Therefore, Jews are cautioned in many laws concerning their reverence that they must have

---

[28] Isaac Jacob Reines, *Sharay Orah*, p. 22.
[29] *Ibid.*, p. 24.
[30] *Ibid.*, p. 25.

upon their entering and their presence within the synagogue. Even when Jews leave the synagogue they are cautioned not to leave in a hurry lest it would appear that they think of it as a burden for their daily pursuits. As the Talmud often states: Let us run to the knowledge of G-d. Commenting upon this verse the Rabbis declared that even on the Sabbath when one should walk slowly he must hasten quickly to the synagogue for worshipping G-d.[31]

Jews are cautioned in Scripture that Aaron should not come all the time to the Sanctuary. The Rabbis infer from this that it is a measure of caution necessitated for the prevention of frivolity and levity. When one is accustomed to a particular mode of behavior he becomes so accustomed with its sanctity that it becomes for him a matter of fact procedure. Therefore Aaron was warned upon the Sanctuary that he must be always aware of G-d's awesome holiness and then he would always feel the ultimate within his capacity to be completely dedicated unto G-d.[32]

Reines, aware of the polemics issued by the reform contingent of Judaism, seeks to defend this seemingly unruly behavior of orthodox Jews in the synagogue. There are two categories of domicile—one, a permanent place; two, temporary living quarters. Those who are only content with the mere lip service attendance to the synagogue naturally are interested in the proper decorum within the synagogue. The refined behavior of the modern movement is not a sign of supreme devotion to G-d. It is rather an imitation of the etiquette and performance of the gentile people. While it is truly appalling that religious Jews act in a manner that is irreverent unto G-d, nevertheless they may understand the mitigating factor arising from the situation of their behavior because those religious Jews are always present in the synagogue. This permanence at times diminishes from the awesomeness of the Sanctuary. The religious Jew feels that the synagogue is a second home. Hence those who are seek-

---

[31] Isaac Jacob Reines, *Or Shivat Ha-Yomim*, p. 27.
[32] *Ibid.*, p. 29.

ing to belittle him would twist and invert the purpose of his outburst and his seemingly irreverent behavior.[33]

Jews must always be equipped with a two-fold aspect of devotion within their prayer. First they must open their mouths as it were to utter the prayers and blessings with holiness. Then they must open their hearts to adjust the intent and desire of their hearts with what we are praying. The phrase *lishkov al dalsosi* is taken to mean the two openings that man must be equally fervent with his heart and mouth to feel the complete sense of devotion to G-d.[34]

Prayer is essential for the development of one's spiritual soul. We know that in time of strife we turn to prayer. This is the means by which we attempt to avert the ill-fated decree upon us.[35]

With all my bones shall I declare unto G-d my devotion for His essence. The phrase therefore means that with my prayer I must be completely filled with the proper devotion for G-d's awesomeness.[36]

The Rabbis were keenly aware of the necessity that one should be able to understand fully what he is praying. They commented in *Sotah*: Prayer is said in all languages. Rashi explains this is to evoke an emotional response to G-d. Therefore the pathos of prayer must contain a knowledge of it. Perhaps it is the result of a lack of understanding of prayer on behalf of the populace that causes them to act in a frivolous manner in time of prayer. The reason why they constantly seek to converse with their brethren is a concommitant of their ignorance of prayer. Reines takes pleasure in his acknowledgment of the translation of the *siddur minhas yehuda*.

The cognizance of one's personal dignity causes him to be aware of recognizing and appreciating a favor bestowed upon him by his brethren. If I can properly express my appreciation for a friend's favor then my own personal character becomes elevated. The appreciation of my neighbor's noble acts is a

---

[33] *Ibid.*, p. 30.
[34] Isaac Jacob Reines, *Or Chodosh Al Zion*, p. 53.
[35] *Ibid.*, p. 54.
[36] *Ibid.*, p. 55.

force that will uplift my character. Not only will I derive physical pleasure but also sublime spiritual fulfillment. As the Midrash puts it: All the sacrifices are destined to become nullified and void except the sacrifice that is identified with a thanksgiving offering. All the prayers will also become null and void except those that are designated as an expression of thanksgiving to G-d. The idea being that the recognition to express one's gratitude comes from the innermost region of the heart. Giving thanks is a result of a sincere emotional expression, hence as long as man is alive this offering and this prayer of thanks shall never be nullified.[37]

The abandonment of *regesh* is the beginning of disillusion and despair. If one loses an object he begins to dwell upon it and finally he gives up all hope of ever retrieving it. If one is concerned with his material objects and his material well-being he is always interested to have them within his possession. Similarly the emotional fervor and the spirit for his religious ideal must always be kept alive, never abandoned, never lost. As soon as the spirit and the drive for one's religious identity begins to slip away from him then his whole personality is filled with an irreplaceable void. If trouble will ensue him he cannot survive. If he is befallen with peril he will not have the courage to meet the challenge.[38]

The Rabbis were keenly aware of the preservation of *regesh* throughout their constant historical travail in the Diaspora. They knew that as soon as the emotional ties for the nation would evaporate there could no longer be a Jewish people. Therefore they set aside a significant day, a day of fasting and prayer, a day of repentance and solemn assembly to convene the people thereby communicating to the Jews the idea of national solidarity. The torment of the ninth day of Ab is that day of remembrance that brings about the outpouring of human emotions. This day which expresses itself with bitter weeping and tragic historic feelings serves as an emotional spark to unite the Jews in the face of all danger. It reminds them of prior

---

[37] Isaac Jacob Reines, *Orah V'Simchah*, p. 4.
[38] Isaac Jacob Reines, *Noad Shel Dimos*, p. 25.

glory and future harmony. It is that historic event in time that evokes the bitter feeling transcending it to a sublime idea of national redemption.[39]

The stream of tears transformed themselves into a stream of salvation. The idea being that the flow of tears is compared to removing the heavy stone from one's heart. On this awesome day the Jew has the opportunity to pour out his heart before his Maker.[40]

This day is a true testimony for Jewish existence despite the tragedy that has torn them asunder. With one eye Jews weep bitterly while with the other they look and hope that a time will come when national sovereignty will be resurrected. This is a true sign that Jews are vibrant for only something that is dead is not remembered hence if Jews attest to the tragic moment then there is the hope that beyond the dark horizon of their exile lies the awaiting dawn of their national restoration. He who does not take part in the mourning, grief and sorrow of the destruction of Jerusalem will not be afforded the right to take part in the joy of its rebuilding and the pride of its reconstruction. One who disassociates himself from joining in communal sorrow is likened unto a dead limb within the corpus of the national body. He demonstrates thereby that he has cut himself off from the community, therefore when the community experiences the time of joy and rejuvenation that one will fall away and die because he was not concerned with *midah k'neged midah*. In the manner that he dealt with the his people's national survival. This is what the Rabbis term nation, namely cutting himself off from communal involvement, so too will the community cut him off from reaping the fruits of joy.[41]

The man who is endowed with material abundance is not eager to separate himself and to part with his possessions. Moreover, one takes pride in one measure of his own object more than nine measures of his fellow's object. When a person sells an object the seller is saddened while the buyer is gladdened.

---

[39] *Ibid.*, p. 26.
[40] *Ibid.*, p. 34.
[41] *Ibid.*, p. 35.

There is an emotional tie between man and his belongings. Just as a man is tenacious in his severance of material possessions so also is he bound to his spiritual possession.[42]

The emotional involvement between the Jew and his land is of extreme importance. Upon your walls of Jerusalem have I appointed watchmen. These guardians are to awaken and quicken the hope and desire for the resettlement of the Jewish homeland. "Such watchmen," he declares, "I have appointed for all time." They are to give the Almighty no rest till He reestablishes Jerusalem and makes it praiseworthy throughout the world.[43] You shall revive with money the desolate Zion. Filled with emotional intent the Jew must always be prepared to carry out his emotion to its concrete and definitive goals. Never shall Zion lie without guardians of hope, without its yearning watchful waiters, when that great day will come and Almighty G-d will revive and rebuild Zion. This watchfulness has been communicated to each and every Jew for we are all her watchmen, we are all her guardians waiting anxiously to fulfill our desire, to make a reality the dream of a renewed homeland.[44]

Whoever lives in the Diaspora is considered as if he has no G-d, and the converse whoever lives in Israel is considered a believer in G-d. Reines takes this passage in the Talmud *Ksuvot* in a metaphorical sense. He who makes his domicile away from the boundaries of Israel tends to arouse the notion that he does not have any emotional desire to see the restoration of Israel. Hence it is not the act of living beyond the borders per se and the geographical location exclusive of Israel that makes one a disbeliever. It is rather that if one lives in Israel he is filled with the emotional attachment for his homeland. The Diaspora is not the place for achieving the degree of attachment to Israel that is so vital for every Jew. Although Jews live outside of Israel their emotional attachment must be turned toward the goal of achieving its settlement.[45]

---

[42] Isaac Jacob Reines, *Or Chodosh Al Zion*, p. 42.
[43] Isaiah, Chapter LXII.
[44] Isaac Jacob Reines, *Sefer Harochim*, pp. 154-155.
[45] Isaac Jacob Reines, *Or Chodosh Al Zion*, p. 44.

The elements that make up a nation are four—language, family, culture and a homeland. The first three are intrinsically concerned with the inner structure and inner growth of a people. The element of a homeland is an external feature that serves as a container wherein the aforementioned three are placed. Although the homeland for Reines is an external feature he hastens to add that it is superior to the others. Without it one cannot envisage neither family nor language nor culture.[46]

The loss of the feeling for Jewish national pride is the less of the essence of the individual. In exile the way by which one can maintain his national survival is with the *regesh* of *tikva*, hope. This hope is indeed a most vital force to preserve the idea of the Jewish nation.[47]

### INTERNALISM AND EXTERNALISM

The main conception of the Torah is to seek and discern the inner construction that binds or separates one law from another. The search for the inner meaning therefore is at the core of the entire structure of intellectual humane pursuits. Shamai and Hillel *elu v'elu divre E-Lo-him chaim*. Both schools, however, varying they are in the Halachah, nevertheless utter words of the G-d of life. Both have the same intent to seek the truth of the law.[48]

The faculty of one's capacity to remember a specific idea is to imagine and equate one set of circumstances to another, one law to another or one fact to another. Although this method may seem conclusive we must analyze the internal structure of the equation. Any fact or any law that we equate with another is like a person who is clothed with a mantel. At times the cloak fits the person while at times we must discern between the *lovesh* and *l'vush*. Hence the capacity to equate and discern within a specific context is derived from the idea of distinguishing or equating of two given hypotheses.[49]

---

[46] *Ibid.*, p. 112.
[47] *Ibid.*, p. 114.
[48] Isaac Jacob Reines, *Sefer Harochim*, pp. 206-208.
[49] Isaac Jacob Reines, *Or Chodosh Al Zion*, p. 84.

Every aspect within the structure of man's being has two approaches. Just as the eye is an external physical object having the internal quality of sight, similarly all of life is garbed with a two-fold looking glass. We can also seek to investigate and grope to find the inner meaning of a particular thing. The simple man or the masses are satisfied with external features and appearance of all phenomena in life. The intellectual man and the elite are more critical, more analytical. They are interested in separating the wheat from the chaff. The organism of the human being is divided into two structures having sensate and cognate functions. The sense organs of a person visualize only the external phenomena while man's rational faculty perceives and penetrates the internal structure about him. External phenomena is separate—one fact being isolated from another while the man who is preoccupied with internal causation of phenomena discerns unity and recognizes solidarity within nature, himself and his fellowman. There are two kinds of association that one has with his fellowman. His companionship could be one of an external nature or of an internal one. An external friendship is casual and the acquaintance is only superficial. As we know when we meet a neighbor we ask, "How's the weather?" An internal friendship however is quite distinct. The friends are deeply concerned for one another and moreover they are involved in their mutual plight. Hence *hishtat fut penimi* is inexorably intertwined with *regesh penimi* a mutual understanding for one another.[50]

Man's function in this world is to unite the senses with his rational faculties. The senses are static and his mental capacity is dynamic. The sense organs cannot create while the rational function in man's mind is essentially only for creating. The object of man in this world is to combine and fuse both the static and dynamic aspects of nature and to incorporate them within his own personality. The Torah is the tool of elasticity that harmonizes this duality within man. The Torah gives man a sense of direction and guides him to a creative and purposeful

---

[50] Isaac Jacob Reines, *Sefer Harochim*, p. 147.

life wherein he can develop himself and thereby completely fulfill his intellectual and spiritual potential.[51]

The body and soul within man contrast and harmonize with one another. Just as body and soul represent external and internal features within man similarly all of nature mirrors the human being. It contains the dual aspect of matter and form, subject and object, spirit and flesh. How does man differ from his fellowman? This can only be achieved through an internal distinction, namely, is A superior in intellect or is A more ethical than B? Height, weight and manner of appearance are not real methods of distinction between man and his fellowman. The method of distinction is by way of internal and intellectual discernment.

If one cannot appreciate and sublimate the beauty of nature within his own spirit then his life is void. Nature must reflect the desire for man to become nigh unto G-d. He who is only concerned with the external and superficial beauty of nature never penetrates the inner hall *traklin* but always remains in the outer corridor. He is compared unto the tree that does not give off fruit. The Rabbis were concerned with an interest in nature that bears fruit. *Etz pri,* they declared, is a tree of nature that culminates into intellectual and spiritual fruition.[52]

The relationship between the internal and the external factors of a particular problem is equivalent to one who is seeking the goals and the means of a particular situation. The means are external matter while the goals are internal matter. When we try to examine the Jewish problem of survival among the nations we should be concerned if Judaism is deteriorating externally or whether the process of deterioration can no longer be remedied. And he smelled the scents of his clothes and behold Isaac declared, "The voice is the voice of Jacob and the hands are the hands of Esau." So long as the hands appear to be like Esau's then there is hope that the Jewish people shall ultimately see the glow of G-dliness. The day of atonement is indeed a symbolic moment as the Midrash relates: It is good

---

[51] Isaac Jacob Reines, *Orah V'Simchah,* p. 68.
[52] Isaac Jacob Reines, *Chosem Tochnio,* p. 38.

for thy children. It shall cleanse them from external iniquity for internally their heart is innocent of sin. If a man has internalized principles his personality is inclined to a conceptual form of development. Then he can become impressed with the precepts of our faith. The elements of perfection within man are three-fold—perfection of body, of soul and of dominion. The perfection of spirit of course is preeminent in man's search for his ultimate understanding of G-d. As Jeremiah exclaimed: "It is like a fire that consumes my innermost being." A step lower in man's gradation of seeking perfection for the G-d idea is the care for his bodily welfare. Last is the acquisition of material wealth which is completely apart from man's person which he must sublimate if he is to cleave unto G-d.

It is a rule in nature and law that the fact which is secluded from our knowledge and understanding requires a maximum amount of contemplation while an object of nature or a fact of law that is apparent to the naked eye does not require great thinking. Hence the external and visible does not require an analytical conception of thought while the internal concept is extremely difficult and requires penetration of thought to reveal its idea.[53]

There are two kinds of treachery. One is open and apparent —the other is hidden and concealed. There are people who use the law as a mantel and garb for disguising their vicious character as we note: G-d, protect me from my friends, of my enemies I shall be aware. It is that hidden deceit that causes many cultural casualties.[54]

History can recount in an extremely vivid form the great tragedies that have occurred by waving the flag of piety. Countless people have been killed for the sake of a so-called cause, while beneath that cause lay great destructive forces to uproot humanity. In contrast, there are men of great piety who appear to be as laymen, simple-minded and unsophisticated, while internally they are deeply pious and possess an extreme reverence for G-d. As the Talmud relates: G-d saw that the righteous are

---

[53] *Ibid.*, p. 41.
[54] Isaac Jacob Reines, *Sefer Harochim*, p. 42.

few so he assessed a fixed number of righteous people for every generation. The wholeness of the righteous shall guide them despite the obstructions they may encounter. Although at times they are confronted with many problems nevertheless since their external behavior is always identical with their internal feelings they shall eventually reach their glorious goal. The treacherous one who constantly looks to deceive and to lead astray his fellow man through his acts of hypocrisy shall eventually become entrapped by his own cunning. *V'selef bogdim yeshudaim.* The deceitful one shall be ensnared by his own treachery. The Halachah requires perfection for example the slaughtering knife for preparing kosher meat. (Jews are forbidden to permit even the slightest blemish on the knife.) This is to indicate that Jews must be extremely meticulous within the scope of practical Halachah. Similarly within the frame of our ethical outlook upon life we must confine ourselves within the fine line of maintaining a high standard of ethics. Jews must be extremely cautious in their conduct and refine their ways to walk upright before G-d. The Talmud expresses great disgust with anyone who seeks to exploit the resources of charity. Anyone who takes money unnecessarily is abhorred by the Rabbis. His heart should be filled with a sensitivity for seeking employment and not to be beholden to the charity box.[55]

As we have mentioned, one of the aspects of perfection that is so vital for one's self-fulfillment is the proper concern for material welfare. The Rabbis have condemned one who seeks to monopolize his fellow man's trade. He who tries to acquire his fellow man's livelihood is likened unto a contaminator of his friend's wife. The abomination of exploiting your fellow man's economic potential is similar to defiling his person. Therefore we must be highly cautious when we deal even on an economic level with our neighbors although we have stated that economics is separate and apart from direct bodily injury. It is however a vital necessity for man's viability throughout his life.[56]

---

[55] Isaac Jacob Reines, *Orim Gedolim*, p. 64.
[56] *Ibid.*, p. 65.

There are three reasons that arouse a man to perform the noble act of giving charity to his poor fellow man. If one cannot withstand the suffering and pain of his fellow man's lack of self-support then he is overpowered with pity and lends his helping hand to that poor man. The second reason is that he feels obligated from a religious point of view. He feels duty bound as a religious person to lend a helping hand to the needy. The third reason is a supreme recognition that every man is created in the image of G-d. The mitzvoh which is the pure religious act is the synthesis between the first and third levels of charity—namely, it is the bridge between pity and dignity for one's fellow man.[57]

Pity is an expression of the emotion while dignity is an expression of the soul. He who gives because of pity is moved perhaps only in response to his emotion. However, he who gives because of the cognizance of the dignity of the individual is expressing the dynamic feeling of the soul.[58]

Abraham, as our sages tell us, pursued the path of *tzadaka*. He was not complacent with donating charity upon the request of the poor, rather he was diligent in seeking out the needy aiming to ameliorate the plight of the unfortunate.[59]

Pity is an animalistic expression for one has mercy on animals. However, love is the expression of a human being. It is love that gives rise to the dignity of man and not pity. Pity is the phrase that is used when we cannot bear the torture of an animal. Love is the humane expression of the *tzelem Elohim* that was endowed to man.[60]

Those who give charity and have the financial means to donate money to their fellow man should be reminded of the contract between Isaschar and Zebulon. The contract is symbolic of true recognition of the personal dignity between man and his fellow man.[61]

"Roll out the scroll of history," declares Reines, "Let us re-

---

[57] Isaac Jacob Reines, *Or Shivat Ha-Yomim*, p. 44.
[58] Isaac Jacob Reines, *Sefer Herochim*, pp. 81-83.
[59] *Ibid.*, pp. 138-140.
[60] *Ibid.*
[61] *Ibid.*

view the historical process of our people. Who are those whom we remember, who can place their names in the everlasting book of noble deeds? They are not the men of material wealth who have been only concerned with themselves—their glorification and their aggrandizement." Only those who are deeply concerned with the maintenance of the spiritual life of the whole community will be recounted and forever cherished. Now why shall we cry for those rich who are merely preoccupied with their own self-interests? Let us cry however for those people who have suffered from those niggardly individuals.[62]

When a person reaches old age he can have satisfaction only if he has matured intellectually. When is *shiva* classified as an ornament of beauty for the head? Only if maturity can be accompanied by longevity. Thus the simile introduced by the Rabbis identifying the term *zokouoh*—he who has acquired knowledge. The time that one has spent experiencing life must culminate in an intellectual and spiritual fruition.

What is the benefit of man for all his toil that he shall invest throughout his life? Man does not benefit, however, civilization which is the continuum of our social cultural heritage, shall reap the harvest of man's toil. It is precisely society who shall benefit hence transferring it to other men. We note here where the antithesis of the individual I, and the collective we, merge and transplant one another. The idea being that each generation forms a thesis and the individual an antithesis. When that generation terminates it becomes a new synthesis for new cultural achievement. (It is quite probable that the entire book of Koheleth is viewed by Reines in a Hegelian conceptual scheme with one polarity against another and one duality transforming into another.) Generations come and generations go and civilization shall forever remain. A time for birth and a time for death—a time for positive construction and a time for negative annihilation.

The mitzvohs concerning man and his fellow man demonstrate the supreme value and high regard that each Jew feels for man in society. This appreciation is an awareness of the

---

[62] Isaac Jacob Reines, *Noad Shel Dimos*, p. 54.

necessity for men to live together harmoniously within the social system. However we should contrast the attributes of man and animal. Animal life is not dependent upon social nexus—animals are rather a biological aggregate that at times cluster together and can be separated. Human beings however are necessarily interdependent upon one another. The natural laws of society govern them to realize and appreciate the value of the human being.[63]

The Torah has forever held precious the preservation of life. We find it replete with countless tannaitic dictum that declare quite succinctly that safeguarding one's life is rooted within the essence of Halachah. "And you shall watch over your soul," teach the Rabbis. You shall protect your person is interpreted to mean caring about your proper physical well-being. One is forbidden to inflict physical harm upon his own person. He who takes upon himself to fast constantly is condemned as a sinner in the eyes of the Tannaim. The Nazarite who abstains from wine is also considered a violator of the true spirit of the law. The aforementioned laws concerning bodily health are just a minutiae of detail that depict the concept of maintaining physical health. Hence the Rabbis were keenly aware that for man's supreme purpose of spiritual devotion to G-d, it is a necessary and vital function to be physically healthy.[64]

The holidays, namely Passover, Shovuoth and Succoth, coincide with various agricultural periods of crop-raising. This is no slight occurrence of mere casual coincidence. It has a rather concrete and definitive purpose, namely, to instruct man that working and tilling the soil are highly regarded within the scope of a true Torah life. Man should take pride in working on the soil as Jews are familiar with all the precepts that are contingent upon the very acquisition of land in Israel. Hence the motif of the precepts concerned with agriculture, and moreover the holidays that are symbolic of a highly developed agricultural life, are aimed at impressing man that he should be

---

[63] Isaac Jacob Reines, *Sefer Harochim*, p. 6.
[64] Isaac Jacob Reines, *Or Shivat Ha-Yomim*, p. 4.

concerned with the acquisition of Israel, planting therein, harvesting and reaping the fruits of his labor.[65]

Commenting on the verse "G-d alone shall lead them and with Him is no strange god," the Sifre implies that those who engage in commercial enterprise are likened to those who would serve strange gods. Reines is very impressed with the physical labors of the individual preempting them over participating in commercial affairs. "Agricultural work," he says, "is sweet and peaceful, simple and direct for the person while the occupation of business trade incurs a good deal of chicanery that leads to the corruption of the human being." (Perhaps Reines was so intent upon his course of criticism as a means of inspiring man to resettle the Jewish homeland.) People should not be smug in their luft professions for the renewal of the homeland is more vital and moreover an imperative for national survival. Those who sow with tears shall reap with joy is not just an aphorism. It is moreover an expression of man's development in his productive and useful life. There is a nexus between patience and achievement. The more a person deliberates and is determined to toil in his daily livelihood, the more meaningful and fulfilling his life becomes. Reines sees a cause and effect between patience for a particular labor and man's desire to succeed with it. They are interrelated and both affect each other. If a person succeeds he has patience to endure and if he has patience to endure he will ultimately succeed.[66]

The person who needs more protection is more prone to incur danger. Hence the person who requires a greater degree of protection and preservation is apt to be confronted with more peril and prone to more injury than he who does not require that degree of protection. (We may inject here that the scholar or man of great virtue is greatly susceptible to those forces that tend to mislead and misguide him, more so than the layman. As the Rabbis noted that he who is greater than his fellow in knowledge has also a greater inclination for evil desires.)

---

[65] R. Werfel, "Netzach Israel—Mamor Chibat Zion," *Sinai*, III (1937), p. 364.

[66] Isaac Jacob Reines, *Shnei Hamoros*, p. 38.

As we have noted there are two basic categories within the sphere of the mitzvohs, commandments between man and man, and man to G-d. Reines contends that those precepts concerning the relationship between man and his fellow are simpler and require less intellectual analysis. The precepts between man and G-d however, since their rationale is much more removed from the ordinary intellect requires that we improve and sharpen our method of analysis and inquiry of those problems that concern man and G-d. Although the mitzvohs between man and his neighbor requires less intellectual scrutiny than those concerning G-d, nevertheless if man transgresses and violates those tenets against his peers the atonement necessary is far greater than if man merely sins against G-d. We are all familiar with the classic dictum in the Talmud—before man can ask of G-d's forgiveness for his iniquities he must at first ask that his fellowman forgive him. He who sins against his neighbor commits a two-fold transgression against man and G-d while the sin which is merely against G-d is a private and singular one.[67]

We can perhaps realize the idea of washing one's hands before one sits down to eat his daily meal—the idea being that before man embarks upon his bodily pleasures to satiate himself he should be aware of any atrocity that he may have committed toward his fellow man. Washing one's hands is symbolic of man's realization of his own behavior for at times he corrupts himself and uses his fellow man as a means towards reaching his own ends. Therefore the washing custom symbolizes the necessity to appreciate the character and dignity of your fellow man.

The respect for the spiritual serenity of man is implicit within the second tablets that were given to Moses. On the first tablet were read laws concerning the observance of the Sabbath that should be remembered as a day on which G-d rested from his creation and thereby sanctified it from all others. In the second tablet the reason for its observance is given as a spiritual day of rest for man that he should remember thereby that he

---

[67] Isaac Jacob Reines, *Sefer Harochim,* pp. 67-68.

was a servant in Egypt. Hence the Sabbath is a day of spiritual rest and cessation of labor for all, including, man, slave and even animal. The purpose of the second tablet is to amplify upon the first, expressing its meaning for the purpose of creation can only be realized if man can become a greater spiritual being. Thus the purpose of the Sabbath is to elevate man to the degree where he can be a free person—free in the sense that he should declare his being as spiritual sovereignty within himself.[68]

You shall love your neighbor like yourself is indeed difficult to comprehend. However, the Baal Shem Tov quoted by Reines gives the interpretation in the following manner. Just as you have faults and virtues similarly you should be able to appreciate your fellow man despite his faults.[69]

The Torah has aroused our moral conscience not only for our own personal concern but also that we may appreciate and understand the situation of our fellow man. We are required to make any effort and any sacrifice to save and redeem the life and the property of our fellow man. *Hashavat aveda* and *pikuach nefesh* are but two examples that reflect the total concept of our religious obligation and moral concern for our fellow man.[70]

In the spiritual devotion for one truth one needn't feel any contradiction concerning another truth. *Ein emes soteres emes,* is a reconciliation of the dual loyalties problem. One can also resolve the problem of secular and sacred studies with this conception. If man is concerned with the truth all avenues that lead to the road to truth although varying, nevertheless have a particular meeting point wherein they converge with man's personality.[71]

All destruction and evil are rooted within man's hatred and jealousy for humanity. Just as there is no sun without shadows there is no person whom we honor and revere that should not have any opponents and competitors who are envious of him and his position in life. Love however, is the primary force of

---

[68] Isaac Jacob Reines, *Orim Gedolim,* p. 84.
[69] Isaac Jacob Reines, *Sefer Harochim,* pp. 9-10.
[70] Isaac Jacob Reines, *Or Shivat Ha-Yomim,* p. 6.
[71] *Ibid.,* p. 14.

creativity within man. All constructive and creative actions and ideas are nurtured and guided with the emotional impetus of love. Jealousy, lust and self-glorification perhaps also flow from the urge and desire to acquire love for one's particular personality. However, these attributes are a corruption of real love and if one pursues that course he digresses from the true path and inevitably encounters iniquity.[72]

The person who is endowed with an exceptional creative ability always assumes the burdensome responsibility of appreciating and understanding the sorrows of his fellow man. There are, as Reines contends, many great men who have realized this ability within themselves. No one can truly be in a perfect state of happiness since he should be involved and concerned with the plight and suffering of his fellow man.[73]

The man who is a truly spiritual being will always recognize and be aware of his fellow man who bestows a favor upon him. *Hacoras tova* is not a required act that is necessary for the recipient of the favor. It is, however, an expression of a deep sense of thanks that impels one to reward his fellow man even though he does not expect his thanks. Although the non-recognition of a good deed done by a friend is not an act of transgression per se nevertheless, it constitutes a serious offense of moral depravity. The honoring of one's friend is a recognition which arises from the *regesh* of man's expression of devotion to his fellow man.[74]

The Rabbis were keenly aware of recognition on one's part for receiving a favor. They often preached sermons for the honor of the inn-keeper to glorify the hotel where they lodged. The recognition of G-d, the recognition of man's soul and the recognition of the human being is obliged to suffer martyrdom. We can ascertain the depths of the dictum that hatred of mankind is a more atrocious sin than those three, namely, adultery, idolatry and murder. For the second Temple was destroyed without any tidings of restoration while the first Temple lasted seventy years. The answer was given by the Rabbis—because

---

[72] Isaac Jacob Reines, *Sharay Orah*, p. 5.
[73] Isaac Jacob Reines, *Sefer Harochim*, pp. 249-251.
[74] *Ibid.*, pp. 189-191.

the second constituted a more destructive crime of debasement of character, namely, *sinas chinom*. Futile hatred is spiritual slaughter that annihilates and disintegrates the soul of our brethren.[75]

There are two dicta within the Ethics of Our Fathers that seemingly contradict each other. Rabbi Eleazer HaKopa states that jealousy, lust and glory eject man from this world and Rabbi Jehudah maintains that an evil eye, evil inclination and hatred of mankind are the causes for man's ejection from this world. Reines reconciles the apparent contradiction. The former classifies the causes that lead to man's downfall and demise while the latter counts the effects that lead to man's deterioration and decadence in this world.[76] If man loves himself and is truly concerned with his own self-preservation he will sublimate and transcend all his inclinations, passions and desires that tend to mislead and misguide him. For example, if one has an enemy and this enemy needs him for a particular favor or the enemy seeks to do him a particular favor, one should transcend his natural inclination of hatred for the sincere motivation leading to the ultimate good that lies within every human being.

Reines expresses a plea for solidarity and unity between the two great forces within orthodox Judaism—namely, Chasidim and Mithnagdim. He abhors and detests the inner conflict that has served as a disparate and discordant force within Judaism. There are two categories of war asserts Reines, external and internal war. Nations if caught in a clash with one another, that is to say, an external war will seek to resolve its inner conflicts that have heretofore plagued them. The Jewish nation that is confronted by so many terrifying persecutions should make a really serious attempt to unify its forces or else it will encounter great tragedy. Let us not argue and scuffle about petty prejudice and minute problems that lead to conflicts of interest. Why should we disagree about problems that can only result in discord and disunity? The reconciliation of those intra-

---

[75] *Ibid.*, p. 15.
[76] Isaac Jacob Reines, *Or Shivat Ha-Yomim*, p. 5.

cultural problems is extremely vital in creating a more harmonious Judaism.[77]

There are three divisions of title by which man is called. When a man is born he receives a name from his parents. This is a familial classification that is strictly biological in nature. Another is the name by which his friends and peers identify him. His place in society becomes recognized and established. The name is one of position and elevated rank. However, although his friends praise him profusely nevertheless that praise may be only considered external glitter. While his friends may appreciate him in his presence this honor may be superficial and meaningless. However, there is a final category by which a man assumes his place within the historical book of world civilization. It is precisely the book of *toldos adam*—the record of man's actions and deeds that he has left as a legacy for ongoing civilization. The path of virtues that man leaves behind him will alone tell the story and evaluate him properly. Hence it is not the biological and social position that man creates upon his historical journey in this world. It is, however, the cultural heritage that he deposits in this world that will give immortality to his name.[78]

We find at times a man who is confronted with many bitter and envious opponents that seek to destroy both him and his ideas. When this man has passed on to the world beyond his enemies take a different turn of mind and view him as it were with a new pair of glasses. Such an episode is quite frequent and occurs often within the scheme of individuals who evaluate one another. If the opponents of a man begin to reflect that he was really and truly a man of unique qualities and gifted attributes, this change of mind does not always presuppose vain flattery. Historically speaking, when a person is removed from his peers then his social group begins to reappraise him in a new perspective. The social group becomes filled with sorrow and anguish for indeed there was a man among them who was replete with virtue and a unique standard of ethical behavior.

---

[77] Isaac Jacob Reines, *Chosem Tochnit*, p. 24.
[78] *Ibid.*, p. 27.

(It is hard to tell to whom Reines is referring—perhaps it is a method of expressing his sorrow for those *gedolim* who misconstrued his approach to Judaism.)[79]

### TRUTH AND FALSEHOOD

Truth is everlasting in nature and permanent in scope. The seal of G-d upon humanity and civilization is truth.[80]

Society must be aware of the person who disguises himself as a self-righteous and extremely pious individual. There are people who attempt to deceive society and use G-d's name as a shield for their treacherous ambition to exploit and expunge their brethren. Do not use G-d as a crutch upon which to support your deceiving and scheming acts of malevolence. The *Tanchuma* has identified semantically the words *lo sesaw*—you shall not vow. The Rabbis inverted the word *sesaw* into the word *masaw* expressing the intrinsic concept that man is forbidden to use G-d as a support for his intriguing desires. The Rabbis declared that a robber of a loaf of bread is prohibited from saying the blessing of *hamotzi* for that piece of bread. Hypocrisy is an abomination and degradation of moral character. The Rabbis understood this quite succinctly. The hypocrite who blesses G-d after his vile act of deceiving his fellow man has blasphemed Almighty G-d. The scene of Jacob's sons who plotted to perpetrate the violent act upon Joseph remind us vividly how men garb their sensuous desires of hatred, lust, self-glorification and self-aggrandizement within the cloak of religion and the mantle of sacred puritanism. The Rabbis recount the agonizing scene wherein after the brothers threw Joseph into the pit they gorged themselves with food and drink. Then they wanted to bless G-d for their meal. The hideous act would become transformed into a divine function. Judah spoke up declaring: How can we praise G-d and disguise our treacherous act? The Rabbis displayed an awareness in exposing the shrewd and cunning tactics of Joseph's brothers.[81]

---

[79] Isaac Jacob Reines, *Or Shivat Ha-Yomim*, p. 12.
[80] Isaac Jacob Reines, *Sharay Orah*, p. 18.
[81] Isaac Jacob Reines, *Or Shivat Ha-Yamim*, p. 3.

The Rabbis aroused our conscience concerning treachery and disguised criminal behavior. They asked in *P'sikta Rabbasi* if the sentence *lo sesaw* refers only to promising. Then it becomes superfluous because the Torah has already prohibited false promising and false swearing. *Lo seshawvoo lasheker.* However, we may infer from the sentence *lo sesaw* that one should not clothe himself in *tzitzis* and *tefilin* to act as piously as he might thereby concealing his insidious deeds. The Rabbis went so far as to express themselves in this manner that acting treacherously is even more vile than committing an offense with presumption or intent—*haarawmaw.* They declared: It shall be more *chamor* than *mazid*.[82]

The Biblical injunction that is aimed at securing proper justice for all in litigation is expressed in the prohibition of taking bribes. Do not take a bribe for it veils the eyes of the scholar and it twists the words of the righteous. This two-fold effect expresses itself in thought and in word. The judge is compelled to behave within the guide lines of proper ethics toward his litigants.[83]

You should not contrive to do iniquity in adjudicating the law. The story goes that the people of Sodom fell upon a stranger and robbed him of all his money. However, each one took less than the value of one penny. Exercising the law in such a corrupt and deceiving manner leads to the corrosion of the personality and disintegration of human character of man.[84]

The terms *meila* and *begida* are semantically identified with their philological connotation. *Maal* and *beged* both mean mantle or garment and both denote treachery and deceit. As Zechariah put it: They clothed themselves in a tight mantle only for the purpose of deceiving their fellow man.[85]

A person must be truly committed unto G-d. His external behavior should coincide with his internal thoughts. Also just as the man of great virtue is intellectually and internally striving for perfection, his physical appearance should also be aristo-

---

[82] *Ibid.*
[83] *Ibid.*, p. 4.
[84] *Ibid*, p. 5.
[85] *Ibid.*, p. 6.

cratic and majestic. The men of the Sanhedrin and the leaders of Judaism must present a certain image to impress all people from all walks of life. Therefore, in a world that is filled with ignorant laymen and pseudo-intellectuals the leader must also be dignified in stature and appearance so that his influence prevails in maintaining discipline and order throughout the entire Jewish community.[86]

Man's life is quite distinct from animal life. The animal has completed its development by merely existing biologically. Man, however, has an intellectual and cultural development that elevates him above animal life. Man's perfection is a gradual process that guides him in attaining a spiritual and intellectual goal. How can we recognize a man who has attempted to attain perfection? He can demonstrate this attempt by daily development and constant progress along the course of finding the path to G-dliness. The degenerate man is one who takes pride in the fact that he has already attained full completion of his personal development. The *ish shalem* is not complacent with his sense of self. He is always eager to strive towards the goal of his self-purification. The *ish hashuv* however is content with his lack of feeling and dedication to aspire to a more intellectual and spiritual life. Likewise we can distinguish between a creative generation and a destructive one. A creative age is concerned with nurturing a sense of development for its particular time. The destructive age is merely preoccupied with immoral and unethical activities.[87]

It is a natural law of human development that ultimate good is arrived at only through painstaking effort and self-sacrificing devotion to the tenets of faith. Evil moreover flourishes upon a minute degree of labor. Man does not have to expend his energies towards committing evil.[88]

Reines distinguishes between two aspects of man's toil on this earth. "Man," he declares, "was only created to toil and exert all his energies for the purpose of attaining a higher in-

---

[86] *Ibid.*, p. 7.
[87] Isaac Jacob Reines, *Or Chodosh Al Zion*, p. 64.
[88] Isaac Jacob Reines, *Sefer Harochim*, pp. 248-249.

tellectual and spiritual development." Laboring for man's physical development and material needs however is futile.[89]

Man without a capacity to reason and understand cannot function. However reason alone will not suffice to give man the proper ability to be creative and constructive. Belief is also a necessary element to refind and direct man to attain the ideal goals of his life. Reason alone may lead to destruction and disrupt civilization and culture while faith is the agency of harmony that harnesses man's energies and drives guiding him along the course of spiritual dedication and complete devotion to G-d.[90]

Many rabbis have commented that man has one essential biological difference wherein his species is different from animal life. Man walks upright while the animal creeps. This biological distinction should arouse man's observation as to why he was created in such a manner. Man should always walk upright lifting his head towards the heavenly and spiritual ideals. Hence the advantage within man's physical development is a bio-cultural one.[91]

Man either develops his character in a positive or negative way. However he does not remain in a static condition for he is not living in a vacuum. The Rabbis were quite aware of this phenomenon. They observed that men are equivalent to the grass in the field. Some sprout, others wilt. They either progress or retrogress. However they cannot resign themselves to a static condition. As Proverbs expressed it: The path of the sage is forward to dissuade him from falling into the abyss. Man must direct and channel his intellectual being. He should not remain stationary in his ethical and spiritual development. Each day should be a new step towards a higher goal of intellectual and spiritual purification.[92]

Life is inexorably intertwined with the concept of time. The manner in which man exercises his time in this world is the essence of his life's creativity. Those who express the aphorism

---

[89] Isaac Jacob Reines, *Sharay Orah*, p. 20.
[90] Isaac Jacob Reines, *Orah V'Simchah*, p. 88.
[91] Isaac Jacob Reines, *Sefer Herochim*, p. 25.
[92] Isaac Jacob Reines, *Or Chodosh Al Zion*, p. 68.

that time is money have greatly underestimated the idea of time. Time is more inclusive and exceedingly more dynamic than a mere monetary concern.[93]

The quality of primogeniture is one that takes exceptional precedence within the scope of Halachah. The first-born has more rights than the other children of the family. Why has the Torah elevated the first-born? In other cultures the first-born assumes the position of power and is an expression of physical prowess of his parents. Sanctify unto me all of your first-born is a spiritual conception of primogeniture. It expresses the notion that the first child should be classified on a higher level only because he is the first in time compared to the other children. Since he has preceded the other children in time he must consecrate himself and be more diligent than his brethren in his devotion and dedication to Almighty G-d.[94]

Reines perceives life and death as two curtains that merge a certain point of one's destiny. The whole of man's life-span is a continuum in time. How man is gainfully preoccupied in utilizing the time of his life is considered as threads that are woven into the fabric of his life. Each unit of time weaves and blends itself to form the pattern of man's behavior. This curtain is one that is expressed by time. However, there comes a moment when this curtain of time ascends into another curtain, namely, the everlasting curtain of immortality. Between these two curtains there should be no partition. The first curtain should connect and serve as a purposeful introduction to the curtain that is beyond the rational reach of man.[95]

Man must utilize his time in a spiritual and creative manner. Only then can his life be categorized as a fulfilling and enriching one. However, he who expends his time in futile matters has lived his life in a vacuum of cultural activity. As Koheleth expressed it: Who knows the number of man's days on this earth and how he shall benefit through all the vanity that consumes his life? When can life be classified in terms of a numerical

---

[93] Isaac Jacob Reines, *Sefer Harochim*, pp. 3-6.
[94] Isaac Jacob Reines, *Or Chodosh Al Zion*, p. 28.
[95] Isaac Jacob Reines, *Chosen Tochnit*, p. 22.

value? The man who wastes his time does not have any time. Hence his life is merely naught.[96]

Man's life-span is considered as a shadow of a fleeting bird. Hence all his energy and effort should arouse his desire to be constantly aware that his preoccupation in life should be one of ultimate commitment to G-d.[97]

There are certain commandments which we must obey even at the expense of our lives. Those laws that are bound up with martyrdom are an expression of the real essence of life. If man must be subjected to transgress and violate these precepts then human life must be suspended. Human life can only be valued if we can maintain a religious life. Hence there are three commandments (concerning idolatry, adultery, and murder) that express the notion that at certain times man cannot claim the principle *pikuach nefesh*. His religious values at times supersede the idea of preservation of life.[98]

Rabbi Chanina Ben Tradjan told his disciples upon his assumption of martyrdom that although the margins of the Scroll are being burned the words will hover about the air. Rabbi Chanina intended to transmit to his disciples an intrinsic lesson for man's eternal being. Although the flesh has been broken and destroyed, nevertheless the spirit carries on throughout. If man is to survive it is because of his identification with the intellectual and cultural idea of G-dliness.[99]

Man can cleave unto G-d even though his pursuits contain a constant preoccupation with the mundane material aspects of everyday living. If man devotes more time to the study of Torah or if he aspires to assist those who excel in the study of Torah he can become nigh unto G-d. If he utilizes his material goals to function as a means toward spiritual goals then he has truly transcended the *gashmius* of life into a sublime spiritual *ruchnius* experience transforming thereby his character into a religious personality.[100]

---

[96] Isaac Jacob Reines, *Or Chodosh Al Zion*, p. 74.
[97] *Ibid.*, p. 74.
[98] Isaac Jacob Reines, *Sharay Orah V'Simchah* (Vilna: Rom, 1899), p. 8.
[99] *Ibid.*, p. 221.
[100] Isaac Jacob Reines, *Or Chodosh Al Zion*, p. 41.

# 3

# Views on Jewish Education

It is unquestionable and moreover a credit to the Jewish people that the Torah has been acclaimed with unanimity and celebrated by all the nations of the world in renown and in high esteem. No one has ever denied the greatness and profundity of the Torah.[1] "One declaration has G-d spoken and I have heard two." The two declarations that I have heard are defined by the rabbis as the written law and the oral law. The oral law is intertwined with the written law. They are not separate and apart but rather they complement one another. The oral law which consists of traditions, customs and concepts that are derived from the thirteen principles of Talmudical methodology serve as explanatory tools to interpret and reconcile the written text.[2]

Reines equates the two-fold law, namely the written and the oral to a king who has designated an order to his officers. When a king issues an order to his generals or officers the document however short and however concise it may be is studied with great scrutiny and much deliberation by his officers and counselors. They investigate and belabor each phrase and minute point. The entire document is studied and read with great care and much attention. G-d who is the King of all Kings and who reigns Supreme has delivered the Torah on M. Sinai. Naturally it is imperative upon Jews to study it assiduously and immerse their total being in ascertaining the veracity of the Torah and defining all its concepts within their mental capabilities. The

---

[1] Isaac Jacob Reines, *Chosem Tochnit*, p. 8.
[2] *Ibid.*, p. 10.

Masoretic scholars are endowed with this task namely, to unfold the principles and concepts that are enclosed within the written word. They are neither permitted to decrease nor to increase upon the word of G-d. Their task is only to define and interpret the word of G-d with emotional purity and sacred devotion to His law. They are G-d's officers, entrusted servants who penetrate the inner core of and interpret the substance of his law.[3]

The oral law has upheld the Jews throughout their entire travail in the Diaspora. It is that unifying substance that gives meaning and vitality to the written law. Thus the structure of Jewish organization and communal life is developed through the dynamic interpretation and intellectual creativity that is inherent in the Talmud. The oral law is inexorably bound up with the written. As the branch is inseparable from its roots so is the Talmud intertwined with the Torah. The validity and legal right of interpretation is inferred and quite apparent from the Scripture per se. "You shall slaughter the animal as I have commanded you," presupposes a detailed and definitive outline of all the particulars concerning the proper method of slaughtering an animal. The Torah has enjoined the Jews from turning left or right to whatever the rabbis shall declare and instruct concerning the interpretation of the precept and the character of any ordinance that they will create in order to assure man's adherence to the law. This clause in the Torah gives rise to a vast and unlimited access of developing and enhancing the scope of the Torah according to their observations and insights regarding the law. This is ample proof to indicate the source of an oral law which coincides and parallels the Torah. Why is there a necessity for the entire oral law and if there is validity to its interpretation it should have been explicitly stated. The Torah has incorporated within its literary boundaries an elasticity that would create principles and methodology to guide and lead the Sanhedrin along the course of proper interpretation. It is not the function of the written Torah to encompass every minute situation that will occur for future millennium and for advanced generations beyond its immediate environ-

---

[3] *Ibid.*, p. 11.

ment. The Torah is keenly aware of the infinitude that is inherent within man's mental capacity and intellectual creativity. Therefore, it has reserved the principles and concepts to enlighten and illuminate the rabbis in each specific era that requires its particular character of interpretation.[4]

We find concerning the Torah, that one who violates its law is not penalized nearly as much as one who commits the slightest infraction as prescribed by the oral law. The question arises: how can the oral law supersede and outweigh the penalty of the written law? The oral law is the key that unlocks and unravels the literary scripture and sacred word that is incorporated in the Torah. Without the construction of the oral law the written remains sealed and isolated from one's personal experience. Hence we cannot realize and observe whatever is written if we are not instructed concerning the how of its fulfillment. We can never ascertain or even dream of reaching or possessing the vast treasure and rich spiritual resources that are embodied in the Torah without scriptural interpretation. Hence the essence of the Torah is totally dependent on and completely subordinated to a concise and completely definitive and detailed explanation of the written word. The oral law is the combination of the safe which unfolds all treasures of the written Torah. It is because of that vital combination that its law takes precedence concerning the penal executions of its violators.[5]

The relationship between the oral and the written law is analogous to rational and sensate perceptions of man and also of the soul and the body. The oral law is the soul and the reason while the written is the body and the sensory perceptions of the Divine laws. Even if the world civilizations give their recognition and praise to the Divine law nevertheless this is trivial in comparison to the appreciation of its supreme value and infinite meritorious worth. The oral law is so interdependent with the written as a flame is to coal. As long as Jews can function with the Torah according to the principles and methodology that has been vested in the spiritual arms of the rabbis then the Torah has substance and value. However, without the

---

[4] Isaac Jacob Reines, *Orah V'Simchah*, p. 61.
[5] *Ibid.*, p. 62.

traditional methodological interpretation, the Torah has no life hence the Masoretic guidelines for interpretation are the source of light for direction and only through it can one aspire to become enlightened from the Torah.[6]

Man should always consider his knowledge minute and infinitesimal. All his knowledge, no matter how much he has amassed is like a speck of sand in contrast to a huge mountain that he must ascend. Therefore man must always endeavor to immerse himself in the source of Torah with all the energy that has been granted to him.[7]

The function of the oral law as has previously been stated is to provide a commentary for the written. If the Torah has forbidden Jews to work on the Sabbath how shall the term *melacha* be interpreted? Only the rabbis can properly define for the exact meaning, namely the thirty-nine *malachos*. As another brief example, the Torah has commanded Jews to bind them for a sign on their hands and a signet on their foreheads. How shall we interpret this obscure passage? To what does the sentence refer? The rabbis instructed that this sentence concerns the placing of tefillin on our hand and head and all the intricate details that are involved with the performance of this *mitzva*. Reines expresses his admiration for the second Kuzari written by David Ibn Natar who has given many splendid explanations and cogent reasons for the validation of the oral law redeeming it from its bitter adversaries. The sanctity of the Torah is expressed in its oral profundity to develop concepts and extract many varied details from its principles, components and general structure. The Tur expresses the idea concerning the blessing on the Torah that the phrase relating that He has given us a true Torah denotes the written law and the everlasting life He has implanted in us denotes the oral law. The oral law is likened unto branches that are symbolic of growth, development and continuity. This explanation can clarify for us the seemingly difficult association of Toras emmes with the written and Chayai olam with the oral law. Is it not that the written law is also an everlasting life and should not the reverse

---

[6] Isaac Jacob Reines, *Sharay Orah*, p. 18.
[7] Isaac Jacob Reines, *Chosem Tochnit*, p. 7.

be true that the oral law is truthful? Reines suggests the aforementioned explanation to resolve this problem? The branches that are symbolic of the oral law give the continuity and reveal thereby the veracity of the written law that is symbolic like roots that are imbedded in the soil. One knows that if one has a tree that symbolizes growth and continuity it is an evident truth that there are roots which have sprouted forth to produce a tree with its many branches.

Reines compares the law to the imagery of Jacob's dream. It is a ladder that stands on the ground which is reaching up to the heavens. The law has a two-fold character. It can be made to coincide with the intellectual capabilities of the average man, and yet one can ascend to the ultimate heights of intellectual profundity in grasping the enormity and depth that constitute the vast area of its intricate problems and complicated discourses.[8]

Reines establishes three main strata that cover the entire scope of Talmudical traditions. The source of development for all Talmudic law is inherent and implicit within the written part. Talmudic law constitutes the basic structure and guideposts for direction in all problems that may arise or in any generation. The oral law symbolizes the perfection of Israel. Through it the nation develops and the pride of its intellectual and creative contribution is envisaged by its enhancement. The development of a systematic law demonstrates man's goals and aspirations to perfect his spiritual self. The presence of disputations in the Talmud gives rise to a development of new ideas and further broadens our conceptual schemes with the various problems. Every generation therefore broadens and deepens the spiritual and intellectual horizons of its law. Hence the nation perfects thereby its spiritual soul.[9]

Reines observes the entire system of law as a contrast between generalities and particulars. The Torah is a general structure to the Mishnah. Once the Mishnah has been formed it assumes a generalized literary position for other developments.

---

[8] *Ibid.*, p. 9.
[9] Isaac Jacob Reines, *Orah V'Simchah*, p. 61.

When the Gemorah had been constructed it became a basis of generalized principles for the Gaonic commentary and response. The latter became a broad base for generalized principles in the development of other commentaries. There is a dualism between generality and particularity. When the particulars become refined they are transformed into general concepts to nurture creative ideas for future intellectual fruition.

The Torah has been transmitted to Israel by G-d in its completeness and fullness. The of G-d is complete *tmimah*. We cannot add or increase in the slightest degree any new original ideas. However, the question is apparent for we see many new laws and ordinances are being formed and are designed to fit the needs and purposes of every generation. How can we reconcile this anomaly? The diligent student can originate new concepts only within the context and frame of reference that is inherent in the written law. The written law is structured upon the interpretation of the traditional methods that have been transmitted to the rabbis. As the Talmud notes in *Yevamoth*, whoever declares that he only has Torah doesn't even have that Torah which he professes to possess because without the oral interpretation the written law has no meaning and its value is dissipated. The Talmud in *Shabbas* declares that whoever holds the Torah when he is naked is buried naked. Reines has ingeniously interpreted this passage to convey the idea that Torah without any interpretation or instruction by the rabbis has no cloth or garment to it. It is without any container. Hence the essential context of the written law loses its validity.

Isaiah declares, "Harden the heart of this people and make their ears thick and smart their eyes lest they shall repent." What do these three symbols of repulsing the Jewish people indicate? The Vilna Gaon suggests that the former *hashmen* refers to the mystical and metaphysical portion of the Torah and the deafening of the ears refers to oral law concepts that are transmitted by the traditional principles of hermencutics and the third, smarting of the eyes, refers to the written law. This gradation presupposes the complete disintegration of Jewish culture hence the foundation of the Jewish people disappears. If, however, according to our previous suggestions that without the Torah *shebealpeh,* oral law or without the mystical law there is no basis for Jewish culture, so the third classification, namely the written law has no support or meaning. Therefore, why not leave the Jewish people with the third category? That is, the written law. Why shouldn't the Jewish people remain with the written law? The answer is that as long as they have a spark of the written law they can develop principles and create a new methodology and broaden their culture. Therefore, the evolution of Jewish culture can once again become realized. The prophet wants to completely destroy all hope for the Jewish people in that particular message. As long as we have the spark of creativity that is inherent within the Torah *shebiksav* the Jewish people can resurrect itself for its survival is contingent upon its culture. We observe that all those who are removed from the oral law and only abide by the written have divorced themselves from the essential center of Jewish spiritual survival. Those who have only remained with the Torah *shebiksav,* the written Torah, are daily disintegrating and have no vibrance or dynamism to their cultural creed. The very essence of the Jewish people is contingent upon and determined by developing and systematizing the oral law. The national spirit is determined and motivated by its cultural creativity and intellectual productivity.[10]

All Torah that has no handle cannot maintain itself. Rabbi Azira quoted in the Yerushalmi has expressed this idea to denote that all principles of Torah must be accommodated by examples, because all principles cannot generate any meaning without proper explanation. Hence the example gives color and illuminates the idea that we are trying to explore. The foundation for the excellence of the Jewish nation is premised upon the thought that Jews endeavor to discern the internal principle and inner core of every structure and ideology. All of life's phenomena are understood from an intellectual and critical method. Jews are not merely content with isolated phenomena and great details, but rather to investigate and discern the inner-

---
[10] Isaac Jacob Reines, *Chosem Tochnit,* p. 8.

most idea and to penetrate the inner substance of a particular problem. Hence when Jews examine the inner meaning of a particular problem they try to develop and create a system that should help to solve future problems. From one set of problems Jews derive knowledge to maintain and uphold ourselves when a new problem may arise. So each problem is to be understood in its particular form but moreover we study the principles that guide us to analyze the problem and therefore we can learn and benefit from it for future times.[11]

The rabbis always used this approach when they attempted to grapple with a particular problem. The Talmud says both contentions of dissenting opinions are correct for they had a particular goal in mind—the purpose of arriving at the true halacha. Hence all problems in life are governed by halacha. These problems have a central purpose of direction, an intellectual process guided by a dynamic movement. Indeed, the very term halach is semantically identified and equated with a process of development.[12]

Searching and investigating is the very important and the extreme motivation for halachic process. Rabbis are not content with the simple superficial meaning of any legal concept. Rather they endeavor to uncover and disclose the hidden meaning that is always exploring and defining. This is what the *Sifre* alludes to in *haazino*. There is no portion of the Torah they declare that has not enveloped within itself the resurrection of life, *tchiyas hamasim*. However, we are not equipped with sufficient capability to explore and reveal it. This idea denotes that the Torah has the potential for revealing a higher standard of ethics and the ultimate task is to ascend and always strive for it.[13]

All the words of the Torah are interdependent and mutually related to one another. So declares the Midrash in *Chukos*. These words help to clarify and help to question. We learn thereby to expound on the various problems. The role of the thirteen hermeneutical principles is to provide us with the tools

---

[11] Isaac Jacob Reines, *Sefer Harochim*, p. 124.
[12] *Ibid.*, p. 125.
[13] *Ibid.*, pp. 123-124.

necessary for the derivation of law, concepts and principles. Hence we can only erect an illustrious edifice combining various facts and equating them only if with the right foundation. We must also be capable of discerning and distinguishing between various phenomena and factors that tend to appear similar. The *Yerushalmi* comments that if there is no knowledge how can man possess the awareness of discerning between factors? The eye, Reines comments, perceives thick or heavy objects while the mind is more refined and discerns between phenomena. Hence we must be equipped with the awareness of separating facts from one another. This is the essence of all questions and answers that arise in the Talmud. The *Makshon* or the one who asks the question was equating two phenomena. However, in reality the *Tartzon* reminds the fellow who asked the question that he did not understand for his equation is erroneous and his analogy is based upon a false conception. The dual process of halacha is to equate facts, problems and all of halachic phenomena to one another. People must also be capable of discernment and distinction not to be misled by any allusions of similarity and likeness with the Torah. The compilers of the Talmud stated in metaphorical language that the Torah is identified with gold. As a person exchanges a gold piece for many coins, similarly the Torah has principles that are derived from many particulars. Only if we preserve the gold can we trade for other coins and only if we preserve the essential principles that underscore the centrality of the Torah can we secure all its particulars and maintain the wholeness of the Torah. The Rabbis constantly were aware of the fact that Jews may tend to forget and lose tract of many principles concerned with the oral law. Thus they were eager to arouse awareness for the study of the Mishnah, wherein all the essential principles of the Torah Shebealpeh can be found. Even if Jews forget certain principles then can reconstruct them from the principles established in the Mishnah. Rabbi Akiva, who was perhaps the most renowned of all the Tannaim, was depicted in the Talmud as an *otzer bawloom*—a treasure house of compartments. Rabbi Akiva could store away the various details of all the Talmudical intricacies in the oral law for he compartmentalized the various subject matter which are contained in the Talmud. All the great students of that time assembled to hear Rabbi Akiva for he could systematize and conceptualize all the various phenomena and details in his classical method of sifting the principle from the many facts. If Jews can remember the principles they will inevitably remember all its particulars.[14]

The Torah is only acquired through *Simanim*, symbols of memorization and pneumonical devices created for purposes of memorizing the various intricate details of the problem. The Rabbis declared that 613 Mitzvahs were transmitted to Moses at Sinai and then David came and systematized the Torah on eleven principles, Micah on three, and Habbakuk on one. This is not to say that the Torah has only one required mitzvah. However, the idea of *taryag* and the various other classifications denote the structure of principles—that is, the Torah is the basic blueprint for development and creativity. If we remember the symbols that guide us to understand all the particulars then even in times of persecution and extreme peril when many particulars perhaps will be forgotten or many manuscripts lost, we can reconstruct and reassemble the various particulars because we know the principles—the key issues that give rise to these particulars. We note also that in the case of Othniel ben Knaz the Talmud tells that he restored 900 halachas that were lost in the time of tragedy of Moses' death when the laws were forgotten. Othniel ben Knaz, however, was able to rediscover those halachas with his keen acumen and logical insight into the principles of the Talmud.

There are two categories of creative original thought, namely, a *chidush pruti*—particularized original thought and *chidush klalli*—a generalized creative thought. The Talmud suggests idiomatically that at times we can only rely upon a particular *chidush* in that specific instance. However, we are not permitted to derive from it in the solution of future problems. Needless to say, the generalized *chidush* stimulates creativity for further original thought.[15]

---

[14] Isaac Jacob Reines, *Chosen Tochnit*, p. 19.
[15] Isaac Jacob Reines, *Orah V'Simchah*, p. 61.

Better is he who seeks to digest on his own the intricate problems of the Talmud than the fellow who is being spoon fed and who is served on a silver platter as it were the complete law without any kind of self-analysis and investigation into the problem. The Rabbis have termed the scholar *shinena* a fellow who is ingeniously astute in the problems of the Talmud. The term is semantically equated with teeth. Hence the sharp person, the bright student, can digest and chew the difficult passages of the Talmud on his own.[16]

He who departs from his scholarly friend should not leave without transmitting to him an original thought, a creative idea in the Talmud, for he who imparts a new principle and a new thought will generate and motivate other thoughts and other ideas thus he has truly communicated the concept of teaching Torah to his friend.

A generalized principle and a broad categorization that leads to other original thoughts and creative ideas gives continuity to the Talmud and increases the dynamism of the Talmud and does not permit it to remain static. Hence the generalized *chidush* gives dynamism to the Talmudical law while the particularized *chidush* gives rise to static in the Talmud because the particular *chidush* cannot be extended to a greater variety of original thought.[67]

Both aspects and phases of the oral law are necessary and pertinent to the permanence and everlasting quality of Torah *Shebealpeh*, oral law. Jews must regard both as of equal importance. The generalized original thought gives vitality and dynamism to create other *chidushim*, other laws and other principles to guide us along the course of future problems. However, we must also have a bulk of factual and particularized law from which we can classify, systematize and categorize for future concepts and principles and other hypotheses as they may arise. Therefore we have a contrast in our system of law. We have a clash between a general concept and a particular concept. In an increasing flow of cultural creativity the general concept pro-

---
[16] Isaac Jacob Reines, *Or Shivat Ha-Yomim*, p. 24.
[17] Isaac Jacob Reines, *Orah V'Simchah*, p. 63.

duces particularized facts, particular problems and from the particular problems emerge the greater and broader generalizations.

### HALACHA AND AGADAH

Halacha is for the *Tofsay ha Torah,* those elite, while Agadah is reserved for the entire populace. Agadah is the folk tale and the folk lore which is reserved for them. The many intricacies of various discourses are removed from the general populace. However the pleasant stories and the delightful folk lore are very close and very dear to the hearts of the masses. Hence we have a two-fold process of cultural development. There is the halachic structure of intellectual analysis, creative ingenuity motivating the rational faculties and stimulating the logical abilities of man. However, there is another aspect to culture, that is the *regesh,* the emotional drive, the emotional feeling of sparking and igniting the spirit to a higher ethical goal and more elevated moral standard of living.

The Halacha is at times difficult to be ascertained by the populace. However, the multitudes study various legendary portions of the Talmud. As we have seen in many synagogues, those who are more intellectually inclined, study those sections such as *Noshim* and *N'zikin,* laws dealing with marital problems, tort liabilities and basic civil criminal law. The majority of the masses however study the sections concerning *Moed,* laws pertaining to the holidays and synagogal material.

Agadah consists of the language of emotion, while Halacha is predominantly the language of logic. Hence the function of Agadah is to motivate and to stimulate the ethical and moral ideas in the Torah to illuminate and instill within the person the spiritual fervor and religious dynamism. Halacha is intellectual, rational and concise. It does not come into purview of the frame of reference that is reserved to Agadah. The language of Agadah is like a flame of fire and a burning coal that is designed to elevate the people from their spiritual slumber and to extricate them from their moral lethargy. The law, however, the Halacha, is written in a bland language. It does not seek to overpower or to overwhelm one's inner being. It is a cool stream and a steady flow. We can perhaps analogize this to what the prophets have symbolized and metaphorically expressed. "Behold my words are like fire, says the Lord, and like the hammer that will smote the rock." Then in another passage the prophets say, "Behold all who are thirsty come and drink my water." The Torah has been equated to fire and water. We can perhaps use Reines' analogy that the fire of the Torah is the agadic portion to stimulate, to inspire while the water of the Torah is that cool calm flow that the thirsty person drinks and refreshes himself to become calm, sedate. The fire is to extricate the person from his mundane material world and to elevate him to a more sublime spiritual life.[18]

The sermonizer on the pulpit must be aware of the various *midrashim* and be able to utilize them to exact the message that he wishes to communicate to his people. The law, however, is usually reserved to the Talmudim as we have previously stated. So the Talmudim of the Torah, the Talmud Babli and the Yerushalmi is basically the Halachic part, sections that discuss the many Halachic problems. However, the *midrashim* are usually geared for the masses. The homilies that have been discussed on Shabbas perhaps, or on the various holidays instruct and guide the people, the multitudes, how to behave in the proper way and how to be guided by the attitudes prescribed in the Torah. The purpose of Halacha and Agadah and these disciplines are not mutually exclusive nor are they totally irrelevant. They overlap at times and the intellectual scholar who is equipped with the knowledge of both aspects of the Torah should be able to interrelate and merge the two, for the Halacha should also have a certain spark of emotion and the desire to motivate and stimulate one to a higher spiritual goal. Also the Agadah, the homiletical portions are not merely words of poetical praise and only reserved for becoming emotionally devoted to G-d. Agadah likewise has ideas, concepts, and a logical system that govern the ethical and moral systems. It is the task of the leader to blend the two and to give life and vitality to both systems for indeed they complement one another.[19]

---

[18] Isaac Jacob Reines, *Sefer Harochim,* p. 18.
[19] Isaac Jacob Reines, *Orah V'Simchah,* p. 48.

Even Rabbi Shimon Bar Yochai who is the symbol of one who was devoted completely to the halachic system and intellectual rational study of the Torah, nevertheless understood the needs of the ordinary people. He stated that whoever cannot learn or study any portion of the Torah can fulfill his obligation to study by merely reciting the paragraphs of Krishma during the morning and night. He understood that many people could not make the time to study. Or perhaps their abilities are not geared to the study of Torah, since they are limited in their reasoning capacity.[20]

A man should not become despaired nor should he be disillusioned concerning his lack of capacity to understand the Torah. One should try and try again. If he does not succeed at first he should be persistent and totally committed to the ideals of the Torah and eventually he will be able to gain further knowledge and become a student of the law. We know of Rabbi Akiba who witnessed the sight of a hole being bored into a rock by the daily dripping of water. The constant dripping of the water wore down the rock and finally created a hole in it. Rabbi Akiba observing this became amazed and overwhelmed by this sight. He was convinced that although he could not fathom all the intricate problems of the Torah, he must assiduously study and devote all his energy and total capacity to its mastery. As we know, after forty years, Rabbi Akiba became the singular most acclaimed Tannaitic scholar in Jewish history. As the story is related, Rabbi Akiba returned to the study of Torah and once again started to involve himself diligently in the learning process of the Talmud. The term that the Rabbis used to the effect that Rabbi Akiba returned to the law indicates that Rabbi Akiba had tried many times and had failed. However, finally he was overwhelmed by the scene at the rock and at once his personality became transformed into a total being within Torah. We should not despair at our lack of understanding of the Torah. We should not surrender to the blissful state of ignorance, but Jews must assert themselves and diligently dedicate their lives for this study that is indeed the essence of

---

[20] Isaac Jacob Reines, *Or Shivat Ha-Yomim*, p. 33.

Jewish life. A person should not become deceived and misled if he does not appear to have mastered a certain amount of the oral law or if he is not sufficiently equipped to understand the principles of the Talmud. Although it seems to him that he is not progressing in the field of his study, he should not fall into despair, because learning is a daily process and gradually he will develop himself. Only the fool thinks that he must see his immediate gains for the toil that he has spent in a particular study. However, the clever person, the man who is intelligent, will realize that it is a gradual process that involves many long years and a person must subscribe his total being to this study in order that he may ultimately attain the goal of becoming a scholar of the Torah. The Torah is not far away in heaven, neither is it on the other side of the ocean, rather it is close to the individual. Hence the Torah was given to every man that he may be able to understand, develop himself and become a more perfect spiritual being. If you shall seek it like silver and like treasures then you shall understand the reverence for G-d and you will also find the knowledge to its paths. The Torah needs to be searched, to be investigated and explored. Only then can the great hidden treasures be discovered. The voluminous folio of the Talmud attests to it. As a man diligently dedicates himself in business to try and amass great material fortune, so must a person toil in the field of spiritual knowledge and must devote his entire life to reap the fruits from such an avocation. Thus when can a man find and reach the ultimate goal of understanding G-d's path? Only if he devotes his entire being, struggling and striving and becoming immersed and involved with all his energy and capacity to decipher and understand the principles and problems of the Torah and Talmud.

There are two methods of learning, either superficial or through a close scrutiny. Superficial learning has a specific value that is quite important to the study of Torah. Although it is not the finality of its study, nevertheless it still retains sufficient importance to examine its quality. My soul has yearned for the study of Torah. The Rabbis comment that the term is used denoting a choppy or staccato form of learning. The word *geresh—gorsa nofshi letahavau*—is indicative of a choppy kind of study, that is the phase before the student has been able to absorb it in a highly intellectual manner. So the rabbis declare: Let a man study even though he forgets and even though he cannot retain it properly for superficial study of Torah has also a measure of value. As we have seen previously in Rabbi Akiva's early development that he persistently returned to the study of Torah even though it came to him in a very difficult way. The Rabbis however were keenly aware of a deeper type of study and they used the term *dok vtishcoch,* meaning refine and you will seek out the law. The term *dok* is a more highly refined method of eating, that is one chews the food in a very fine manner. We have therefore two categories of study. Both are necessary to uncover the hidden treasures of Jewish cultural development. The superficial knowledge gives one the inspiration to investigate and analyze on a higher intellectual plane.[21]

Adam Harishon, the man who was created on the sixth day and subsequently committed the sin of eating from the *eitz hadaas,* was demoted from his original high standard of knowledge. However, on Saturday he did not experience any false flaws in his creative ability, for the Sabbath itself gives one the intellectual quality that is distinguished from that of the entire week. The Rabbis were keenly aware of this fact and noted that with the beginning of the work week the first blessing to denote the new week begins with the supplication concerning man's quest for knowledge and intellectual ability. However, when Saturday night came, man began to be weary and was overwhelmed and awestricken by the fear of nightfall. He was powerless to confront the problem of man combating darkness. However, G-d prepared Adam two stones and he rubbed them together thereby producing light. The blessing on Saturday night *havdalah*—distinguishes itself with the blessing of the creation of light. It is the very essence of bringing together two facts and developing a thought that is the unique genius and gifted quality that is reserved for man. Man distinguishes him-

---

[21] *Ibid.,* p. 36.

self from all other animals because of his spark of creativity that permits him to create for himself his own environment. Although Adam had lost a good deal of his divinely inspired knowledge, he nevertheless remained with the potential to create his own and with his own sweat he can eat bread. Man's spiritual creativity and his entire intellectual development must also be derived from his own involvement. He alone must be immersed with all his energy and all his capabilities and must be devoted and dedicated to intellectual creativity. This is the idea behind the Midrash concerning Adam's collection of the two stones. It is the creation of principles that gives rise and inspires man to his ultimate goal of creativity. Therein was man made in the image of G-d. This is his purpose and the very essence of his role in life.[22]

A person should be so immersed and so involved in the study of Torah that no pain whatsoever should interrupt him from his course of study. All the inflictions and persecution that man encounters should not mislead him or cause him to digress from the ultimate study of Torah. The Talmud relates an episode concerning Rabbi Eleazer, the son of Shimon, that although he suffered immense pain and great anguish he nevertheless always diligently studied the Torah. His students came to him and he told them, "I must bid you farewell because you will retard my development in the study of Torah and I will not be able to maintain its study." Rabbi Eleazer, who was afflicted with immense torture and a great deal of suffering nevertheless was so immersed in the study of Torah that when he studied he would not feel pain because the emotional quality of the pursuit of one's intellectual study removes suffering.

The Talmud also records an incident concerning Rava that although he had burst a blood vessel on his finger he did not realize this because he was involved in the study of Torah. Hence if one is really diligently devoted to the study of Torah his physical disability almost remarkably disappears. The psychological tensions and anxieties are removed from man when he is ultimately committed to the study of Torah. Rabbi Eleazer

---

[22] Isaac Jacob Reines, *Chosem Tochnit*, p. 17.

did not want to act rudely to his students but he was interested in continuing his studies so that he would forget about his pain. This also is the idea behind the classical maxim that whoever has a pain in his head should involve himself in the study of Torah.[23]

The Rabbis many times clothed their words in an almost indecipherable manner. This is not because they wanted to appear esoteric. They did so however to convey a lesson. Rabbi Zerah maintains that the words of the Rabbis and their riddles are meant to inspire the Jews so that when they finally ascertain the proper meaning of the particular problem they should always retain it. Hence the memory of a particular section or discourse in the law is contingent upon the factor of man's involvement in the problem and his dedication to unraveling its apparent paradox. If one has to deliberate and expound on a particular principle, in the final analysis when he comes to a solution it will remain with him with the entire methodology that lead him to his solution—the method of analysis that he arrived at when he finally concluded his particular proposition.[24]

"All the Torah that I studied with extreme zeal and intense fervor has remained with me," declares the Midrash in Koheleth Rabba. When a man studies with a great deal of love and with an animated desire then this study is preserved in his memory and he will always retain it.[25]

There are two goals wherein one can attain the study of Torah. There is one idea of learning Torah for its very essence —namely, only for the study of Torah per se, not for any external gain or any other ulterior motive. This is the more supreme motivation of study. This is the internal form of creative learning. When one devotes all his time, energy, and capacity to the pure study of the Torah, then he can reach a higher level and ascend a tremendous rung on the ladder of spiritual development. However, if one studies merely for external reasons or any ulterior purposes his Torah is superficial. Indeed if one studies for honor, self-glorification or self-aggran-

---

[23] Isaac Jacob Reines, *Or Shivat Ha-Yomim*, p. 22.
[24] Isaac Jacob Reines, *Orim Gedolim*, p. 49.
[25] Isaac Jacob Reines, *Shnei Hamoros*, p. 19.

dizement he cannot really tackle the problem and many of its facets will be lost to him. He is deceiving himself as long as he feels that he has acquired some knowledge and he is able to boast of it to his friends, neighbors or relatives. His learning task is done and he has no other aspirations. However, he who is not content with merely finding grace in the eyes of his friends will always strive for a higher interpretation. He will never be snared into the entrapment of self-complacency or a smug attitude concerning his cultural development and spiritual aspirations. Thus the Rabbis declared that he who learns without proper reverence for G-d indeed his learning has no meaning, for only if a person has complete reverence for G-d and his motivation is spiritually pure and free from external intervention, only then will he be able to accelerate and enhance his intellectual growth and creative ability in the knowledge of Torah.[26]

The learning process is reserved specifically for seeking the truth. Hence even if one does not arrive at the correct Halacha, nevertheless if his intention and concern is to seek out the truth and to search for the right law his aim is considered to be extremely valuable and highly worthy in the eyes of G-d. The Talmud declares that the words of both, namely, the schools of Shammai and Hillel are the words of the living G-d. It is a fact that the law has been decided according to the school of Hillel. Why then does the Talmud comment on the fact that the words of Shammai are also considered the words of G-d? It is precisely because of this element that searching for the truth is also a truth in itself. Practically the issues must be resolved according to one particular party. There must be certain rules for guidance in evaluating Halacha. It is noteworthy that the dissenting opinion in Jewish Halacha is also considered to be the words of living G-d. Jews are not complacent or satisfied with the majority rule or majority opinion. Rather the Talmud is keenly aware that dissenting opinion is important to the vitality and dynamism of the given law. Thus the Talmud asks why the Mishnah notes a dissenting opinion. The answer given is, perhaps in

---

[26] Isaac Jacob Reines, *Sefer Harochim*, p. 92.

future times, in future generations, that the majority will see the view of the dissenter and consider his opinion to be valid. Although practically speaking, law has pragmatic purpose in mind in presenting the present Halacha, nevertheless there must be cognizance of the fact that because of a given situation that may arise Halacha can be ratified in the eyes of a future court.[27]

The Talmud cautions that whoever declares and expresses his desire and eagerness for one particular discourse and is contemptuous of another runs the risk of having the Torah disappear from him. This individual will lose a great deal of his spiritual treasure and cultural wealth because as has been previously stated, the Torah must be studied purely for its own particular essence and not for any external influences that may arise in one's environment. Hence only if one gives equal attention and his whole appreciation to all of the Talmud, only then can he realize his intellectual growth. However, if one expresses his contempt and disgust for a particular problem or theory in the Talmud then the Torah has lost its intrinsic value. Therefore man should be completely preoccupied with the entire Torah and all of its concepts should be equally esteemed in his eyes.[28]

The Talmud has consistently used the term of war and the idiom of battle depicting complete involvement and total devotion to the study of Torah. Hence they used the phrases— "battle of Torah," and the Torah has been called the "ammunition arsenal to study" and if one studies the Torah he "captures the city." Also the Torah has been identified with the sword. Man must sublimate all his physical desires and his worldly ambitions for the purpose of Torah study. Hence the study of Torah transforms one's personality and elevates his character to a higher ethical plane and moral plateau. Man must utilize all his energy and exert all his animalistic inclinations and biological drives for the sublime religious experience of intellectual growth and spiritual development. To study the Torah assiduously gives one the aspiration for continuity. A man can acquire for himself a good name, and an everlasting name in the

---

[27] Isaac Jacob Reines, *Orah V'Simchah*, p. 64.
[28] Isaac Jacob Reines, *Chosem Tochnit*, p. 94.

intellectual striving for the study of Torah. If we contrast this acquisition of aristocracy to that of a military conquest we can distinguish it quite readily. The man who is interested in military conquest creates great tragedy when he becomes an important soldier. His mighty name in battle causes a great deal of bloodshed and much ruin, plundering and pillaging. However, he who has established for himself a name in the cultural sense has memorialized and made himself an everlasting ideal for future times. The study of Torah is the answer to man's drive for conquest. Man's innate nature for seizing upon objects and trying to devour everything in his sight has been sublimated and transcended into a moral ideal. Hence the ethical mission of the Jew is not to be a warrior in physical battle but rather to be a soldier of G-d. Herein Reines maintains lies the greatness of the Jew that on this battleground no one can defeat him.[29]

When Torah is studied in one's youth it becomes absorbed as if it were in one's blood. Man's whole outlook and entire approach to life's problems becomes a Torah viewing objective. His very fibers and nervous system are structured and directed by the Torah that he has studied. Hence if Jews are involved creatively in their intellectual pursuits then their entire personality becomes transformed into a Torah Jew.[30]

The Torah is a tree of life to all those who ally themselves with it. Many are astounded and dismayed by those who indulge in the study of Torah. They consider one who studies the Torah as a batlan. They moreover are convinced that there is no productivity and creativity involved in its study. However, the Torah is the essence of life. It is the tree of life because it gives man continuity for existence. Man receives direction and guidance from it. It is through the ideal of Torah that Jews can maintain their survival and preserve their identity as a community.[31]

The converse is equally valid—that is, he who neglects the study of Torah leads a futile and useless life. Ezehiah stated that whoever does not immerse himself in the study of Torah

---

[29] Isaac Jacob Reines, *Or Shivat Ha-Yomim*, p. 34.
[30] Isaac Jacob Reines, *Noad Shel Dimos*, p. 15.
[31] Isaac Jacob Reines, *Or Chodosh Al Zion*, p. 180.

shall be slain by the sword. The idea being that to the one who is repelled by the study of Torah life has no meaning. In a metaphorical sense there are many phrases concerning the idea of placing a sword symbolizing that whoever does not study the Torah will be smitten by the sword, as the one who stuck a sword on the threshold of the Bais Hamedresh, because life is a life of Torah, and whoever actively renunciates this kind of life has forfeited his very being.[32]

King David recognized the infinite quality inherent in the Torah. All drives and lusts are limited within a certain boundary, that is to say, they are subjected to various degrees of limitation. "To all purposes in life I have seen the point of termination," remarks King David. However, the study of Torah, is endless in goal and limitless in nature. If there are any drives that appear to be infinite they are only to be sublimated for the cultural study of Torah. "With this idea he will overcome his enemies," remarks King David, for the Torah which is infinite will overpower and overwhelm all limited and finite matter. We may infer from here a kind of tripartite infinity that is inherent in the entire scope of Jewish philosophy, when we contend that G-d, the Torah, and Israel are unified and interwoven by one another. We may conclude that all three have the ingenious quality of infinity, that is, they cannot be limited or they have no point of termination. Thus, all other matter have their point of finitude as can be seen in the coming and going of many cultures. Israel however has survived the many titanic waves that have swept over its boundaries and beleaguered its citizens. Israel will forever stand because it is interwoven with infinity and the quintessence of everlastingness.

Rabbi Shimon Ben Jochai was completely dismayed and much disturbed with those who turn away from the involvement of Torah study and he could not fathom the idea that people can become preoccupied with other mundane material matters and discard their duties and obligations that are ultimately linked with the study of Torah. Moreover, he who devotes and dedicates his whole life to the study of Torah, the *Ethics of Our*

---

[32] Isaac Jacob Reines, *Or Shivat Ha-Yomim*, p. 54.

*Fathers* it is remarked that from him will be removed the burden of military worship and also the toil for daily bread, because one who is involved in the study of Torah uses all his energy and channels his ability towards his toil. Hence the spiritual toil removes physical toil because the essence of man is to aspire to a higher spiritual goal. Therefore, if man is concerned only with the spiritual essence of life G-d shall remove from him the material burdens of life so that he may be able to sufficiently sustain himself in the study of Torah without any external suffering.[33]

How astounding, the Rabbis exclaim, that when one observes the animals one sees that they are never in want of food and they are always satiated. Now man is always hungry and is always craving for food, for bread. Why then can we never imagine a deer being hungry and a lion without bread. The Rabbis admit that our sins have caused the lack of productivity and lack of provisions in daily livelihood. If one would have perfect trust in G-d and completely surrender his material drives to the ideals of intellectual pursuits then he would not have to worry continually about his economic provisions. We have briefly observed how the Torah gives continuity for man in his entire life, not only intellectually but also in the material aspects of life. Hence only the study of Torah can prevail when man confronts the perils of nature and he is challenged by the storms and stresses of foreign influences.

### EDUCATION OF CHILDREN

When G-d gave the Torah on Mount Sinai he asked the Jews: Who is your surety, who can take responsibility that my Torah shall be transmitted to future generations? And who will carry the burden of Torah for a timeless memorial? The destiny of Torah is not to be administered only for one or two or three generations but it is the declaration of human freedom for all historic time and for all problems that may arise in the unforeseen future. The Jews answered that their children will be a

---

[33] Isaac Jacob Reines, *Eduth B'Yaacov,* Sermon III, p. 27.

surety to uphold and maintain, to preserve and to keep the Torah and its mitzvos. The transmission of Torah then to the children, namely future generations, is to maintain the continuity of Torah, to preserve the chain of tradition, to uphold the banner of faith and to retain the tenets of old. The sanctity of the Torah is preserved in the container of youth. From the mouths of babes and sucklings you have established your throne. You have erected your strength, your fortress to defeat the enemy, and those who seek to take vengeance on you. Hence the children, the future generations, are the surety for the preservation of the law for all times. Wherein can we discern that the children will be able to carry on with the ongoing process of maintaining the structure of Judaism in its proper form? Respect for parents is perhaps a symbol *sine qua non* to this idea. When children have a high regard for the parents it denotes that the parents have correctly transmitted the ethical practices and moral teachings that they have adopted for their life-long goals and aspirations.[34]

Many have the impression that with the advent of science a new era of modernity has assumed a place in the sphere of religion. We should now take a different perspective to adhere to the youth because they have the recently acquired methods of empirical knowledge. Reines however refutes this contention because with the Torah, with Judaic culture, Jews base themselves primarily upon tradition, that is on the axioms that have been traditionally communicated and have guided the Jews throughout all times. Pertaining to rational matters Jews owe their allegiance to the time of old, to the Zekainim because they were closer to the masoretic tradition. Only in regard to scientific matters where it lends itself to empiricism may Jews lean or be inclined to believe the present generation. However, the advent of science should not becloud the rational issues of intellectual identification with masoretic traditions.[35]

The concept of tradition has been formulated in the Hebrew phrase *shalsheles hayuchsin*—that is, to denote heredity in the

---

[34] Isaac Jacob Reines, *Sefer Harochim*, pp. 263-264.
[35] Isaac Jacob Reines, *Chosem Tochnit*, p. 15.

framework of a chain. Hence tradition is like a never-ending chain that encompasses all generations. Jews must communicate their principles and make certain that the principles guide them for a historical destiny that is everlasting in nature and timeless in scope. Hence, the literature of the Talmud has semantically identified tradition with the chain. Every generation is seen as father and child—the child is another link in the chain that has been established by the parents. When Jews observe their cultural process in the form of a chain they can readily understand why their goals are unique because of their approach for ascertaining the ultimate ideals for all historic times. Why have Jews maintained themselves during such perilous times in their historic travail? Because they have the view towards the future that as long as the chain of their cultural heritage has not been interrupted and has never been discontinued then they have kindled in their hearts the torch of hope when they aspire toward the ideal time when the ultimate redemption will come to Zion.

In the present time of peril and strife Jews should be cognizant of their obligation to their children, and must endeavor to give them the most beneficial education which in turn will enable them to have the spirit and drive to withstand and weather all the titanic storms and stresses that will confront and challenge them in their undertakings. "Come, take hold of your child," declares the Angel to Hagar. If Jews are to transmit and communicate their principles and Jewish way of life to their children they must give heed to their growth and observe their spiritual development. If a father sees that his child has great potential and gifted qualities he will naturally do his utmost to try and cultivate his talents and channel his energy towards the proper goal and to motivate him to expand all his energy towards the ideals of Torah. We are aware of the Passover service concerning the four children discussed by the author of the Haggadah. The wise son, the wicked son, the simple one and the one with no ideas. Each son must be treated according to his own capabilities. The clever son must be encouraged as far as possible. The wicked son must be ridiculed and chastised without completely abandoning him. The simple one's faculties must be sharpened. Thus we are confronted in life with sons who have varying capabilities and the Torah has instructed Jews to deal with each one on his own level. Much discord and discontent can be eliminated if Jews utilize the metaphorical lesson that has been expressed in the Passover service.[36]

Reines proclaims that we have to be aware of and show great concern for the education and upbringing of the daughters of Zion and the women of Israel. Jews must not neglect their education and must preserve the family purity that has symbolized the solidarity inherent in the Jewish family structure. Jews must establish groups of women and girls who will abide by the law and will nurture and develop the spirit of Torah and the zeal of Zionism. Thus shall you declare to the house of Jacob and make it known to the children of Israel. The Midrash comments that the house of Jacob are the women of Israel. Jews must instruct their women with the necessary knowledge and inculcate them with the spirit of the law. Women are the guardians of children and the protectors of youth. It is true that education is learned in the classroom. However it is the home that gives the child the warmth and the drive to carry on in face of all kinds of conflict. Thus the home environment that the child is brought up in is equally important to the one in which he is exposed during the educational process. The two environments cannot be severed. They are interrelated. There is a nexus between teacher and parent and both overlap. The teacher must be concerned with loving a child and the parent must be equally involved in the spiritual development of his child.[37]

The Midrash was keenly aware of the woman's intuitive power in guiding the child along the proper course of Torah and in motivating him to develop fully his potentialities.[38]

Rabbi Jose declared in Shabbas, "I have never called my wife *ishti* in the particular sense. Rather I have always called her *baisi* my house, my household, my home." The woman does

---
[36] Isaac Jacob Reines, *Sefer Harochim,* pp. 99-104.
[37] Isaac Jacob Reines, *Noad Shel Dimos,* p. 62.
[38] *Ibid.,* p. 63.

not merely function in the role of a wife but rather her task, mission and purpose is to uphold and maintain, to keep and preserve the house, the entire household.

The Rabbis were well aware of the woman's instrumental role in inculcating the love, drive and spirit into the children's hearts. As they noted, they depicted Rabbi Jehoshua Ben Chananya with this classic idiom. Blessed is the one who has given birth to him, *ashrei yelidato*. They realize that to produce such a man and to develop such a personality in Judaism was the result of an excellent woman without whose love and guidance Rabbi Jehoshua could never have attained his full potential and could never have arrived to such a splendid position and eminent degree of scholarship in the annals of the Talmud. Rabbi Chaninah declared that when his mother played with him and told him stories in his youth, this inspired him with the courage to continue his studies and to reach a higher rung in his Torah studies. It is quite apparent that many of the Amoriam and Tannaim in the Talmud felt duty bound to acknowledge their mother's influence in their spiritual development. To assure the mother's care we must see to it that persons should marry their daughters to scholars, because the scholars will discuss and transmit to their wives the tenets of the tradition and the fervor of the faith. The woman when assuming the role of motherhood will be able to communicate this properly to the child. It was the tradition from time immemorial for Jews to endeavor to marry their daughters to scholars. The Talmud declares that one who marries his daughter to a scholar will reap the fruits of spiritual enrichment and will enjoy the cultural fruits that arise from marriage. Prosperity and affluence are temporary values in one's domicile. However what is the charity and righteousness that prevails for eternity and timeless memory? Only the transmission of the ethics of teachers, of fathers, is the communication of the entire intellectual process of learning. The Torah that is taught to children and taught to their children is the righteousness that will prevail and is the everlasting charity that is bequeathed for all generations. Whoever teaches his grandson Torah is considered as if he had received the Torah from Sinai because the one who is concerned to teach his grandson is really interested in the continuity of Torah and in the preservation of the entire Talmud. This then is the very essence of tradition—to have in mind future generations—not merely for one to be content with his own specific generation. Likewise, he who writes the Torah is also considered as if he received it from Sinai because writing the Torah is the preservation of the cultural phenomena that is inherent in the Torah.

One cannot study very many things without a textbook. Hence the Talmud is also in that vein the textbook of Jewish tradition. The entire literature that has come down throughout the ages is within the scope of a sefer Torah. Hence Jews must be concerned with the preservation of both the study of the Torah that is related to the person and also to the perpetuation of the literature. The person and the literature form the inextricable bond that is extremely necessary for the realization of the continuity and perpetuity of the Torah.[39]

The ongoing process of Torah is compared by the Rabbis to the process of nature. Every generation recites the glories of G-d and in every generation is seen G-d's nature and splendor revealing itself. The Rabbis commented about the one who does not have any continuity. They expressly denoted two categories that delineate a disruption in continuity. Either children or students—both are considered vital in the process of development and are necessary to fulfill the chain of tradition. One cannot have students, scholars without population. However, population without scholars will not be able to prevail. Hence they are inextricably intertwined.[40]

There are two perfections that are inherent in man's personality that are necessary for him. One is his own personalized and particularized development that he must aim and strive for complete perfection and also must not be content that he alone is complete and has reached his spiritual fulfillment. He must impart and transmit his perfection and his sense of com-

---
[39] Isaac Jacob Reines, *Sefer Harochim*, pp. 264-267.
[40] Isaac Jacob Reines, *Orah V'Simchah*, p. 37.

pletion to his children and descendants. Jews must not be merely concerned with their children, that is, they must not only be preoccupied with their children's development to the exclusion of their own spiritual growth. A person might say that his children will give him honor and acclaim. This is not the proper attitude that the Torah requires of man. Man must be content only when he has meted out all his effort and exerted all his energy for his own fulfillment and that he has striven for and devoted himself to his children and his descendants.[41]

Man's position in the hereafter is not merely one which is reserved for the world to come but it is also maintained in this temporal world. If a man has proceeded to transmit the Torah to his children or friends then he can assuredly feel that he will be rewarded in the world to come. However, one who has not sought to implant and sow the seeds of Torah for future generations will necessarily tremble before the day of his judgment. Continuity is not merely a personal problem. It must experience itself in mankind as well. Hence man can only be assured of his continuity in the hereafter if he has endeavored to enrich mankind during his lifetime.[42]

Man's twofold perfection, namely his own personal development and his conscientious transmission to his descendants is expressed in the phrase—the righteous shall bloom and blossom like the date tree and the cedar tree. They are rooted in the house of G-d and in the courtyard of their G-d shall they be fruitful. The Talmud denotes this idea implicit in the symbolism of the date and cedar trees. The date tree gives fruit but once the tree is cut asunder it no longer sprouts fruit again. The cedar tree however does not give fruit but if it is chopped down it will rise again. Hence the cedar tree is one's own personal development. One must take care of his own growth and maturity. The date tree symbolizes the idea of transmission and communication to others, namely the fruits that one produces. That is the beneficial characteristic of the date tree. Hence both must be fused and joined by the righteous person.

---

[41] Isaac Jacob Reines, *Eduth B'Yaacov*, Sermon III, p. 26.
[42] *Ibid.*, p. 27.

If one takes care of the treatment of his own development and is conscientious and observant of his descendant's maturity he will be able to be rooted in the house of G-d and be prosperous in attaining continuity and fruition in future generations. When Rabbi Ami ascended to bless the Torah, his colleagues would praise him with the following phrase—that his hope shall be an everlasting memorial for endless time, for generations in eternity—because Rabbi Ami was concerned not only with his own particular growth but the rooting and transplanting of the Torah for future generations. Rabbi Ami and all the classical Jewish leaders were not merely content with being leaders for their own generation nor were they seeking self-glorification and self-aggrandizement. Rabbi Ami was concerned and had the moral responsibility for all times that Torah will never depart from Israel. Rabbi Ami was a man who was completely dedicated and spiritually devoted to the tenets of the Jewish faith and to the ethical code of tradition.[43]

The idea of Abraham's sacrificing of Isaac on the altar symbolizes the supreme task of the father's dedication of the son to G-d. The father must bind his son as a supreme sacrifice unto G-d's both word and deed. Our education must be motivated and guided by the lesson of Abraham's actions even though we are confronted by many perils and problems in our time and age both internal and external. The father must be primarily concerned only with the son's cultural development and spiritual growth. All other problems are secondary and superficial by comparison.[44]

Rabbi Acher in the Talmud remarks about the education of elementary school children. The world stands, according to the sages, on the educational process of the young children of tender school age. G-d alone supervises the education of the children in their early development because now in exile it takes superhuman effort to assume the responsibility of educating children. In prior times when Jews were sitting comfortably and securely on their soil, in Israel, the educational process of the youth was

---
[43] *Ibid.*
[44] Isaac Jacob Reines, *Noad Shel Dimos,* p. 64.

a matter-of-fact situation. It was natural for the elders to educate and instruct the young because they saw that they had to transmit to the ongoing generations the spirit of Torah and the desire for learning. In our times when we are engulfed in a stream of suffering and surrounded by a sea of terror we have to assert our allegiance to G-d and overcome the many obstacles that seem insurmountable. In our times G-d alone supervises the educational process. It is through His grace and goodness that Jews can even imagine a learning process and an educational program for their children, since in these times the tragedy and torment has become unbearable. This not only refers to external problems as we have mentioned before but also refers to the internal dissolution in the Jewish community, that is, the lust and passion for assimilating into the cultural milieu of the secular society. Hence G-d must supervise and G-d alone is the Overseer who gives us the energy and desire to proceed forward to uphold and maintain the principles and tenets of the Jewish faith.[45]

"I will hope and yearn for G-d even though He has covered His countenance from the house of Jacob," declares Isaiah. Even if Jews are confronted with a time of peril and Israel seems to be assimilating in the cultural milieu of foreign influences and adopting the social symbols of the non-Jewish community yet I place my trust and assurance in G-d and I will not lose my courage, nor forfeit my convictions that the civilization of Israel will endure and prevail. The children with whom we study will be the symbol of continuing an ongoing tradition. They are the true testimony for everlasting existence and they will always carry with them the torch of Torah to light and illuminate their way throughout the entire dismal darkness that has engulfed them in the Diaspora.

In the present time Jews must be aware of the educational development of adult laymen. Jews cannot neglect their intellectual development. They must be interested and concerned with the study of Torah and with those who are at the head of the academies, the scholars and great rabbis. Without a class

---

[45] *Ibid.*, p. 65.

of educated laymen Jews cannot develop great scholars and significant rabbis who will be able to interpret and convey the Torah in its proper context and true meaning. The lay class must also necessarily be able to support and be concerned with the needs of scholars. Hence, Jews must acquire the two-fold relationship which is mentioned numerous times in the Talmud —the partnership of Issachar and Zevulun. Issachar was totally involved in the study of Torah while Zevulun was his economic benefactor and supporter. If Jews are to maintain excellence in the study of Torah it is incumbent upon them to have educated laity to inspire them with the recognition of the dignity and value that is ultimately related to and a necessary prerequisite for the cultivation and continuity of scholars and leaders of distinction.

Why hasn't the Jewish community in Germany produced any great literary works in the field of traditional Torah scholarship? Reines answered that the laity is completely ignorant of the principles of law. Moreover they have no concern and a complete disregard for the classical zeal of Torah study. If the Zionists endeavor to change the standard of education then the protestors will have a valid criticism to support their contention that the Zionists are not fulfilling their obligation in the line of Torah. How can the freethinkers shape the policy of education that is reserved only for those who are completely involved in its study? How can the irreligious members of the Zionist movement have the audacity to institute their mode of education that is completely foreign to the spirit and mainstream of traditional Jewish education? Even if it is maintained that the educational reforms are merely pedogogic in nature nevertheless one must be aware of the fact that he is suspect in this regard. One must realize that with reference to the pressures of an educational system Jews must incorporate men who contain the proper respect and reverence for G-d because it is obvious that the freethinkers are divorced from the traditional path of G-d fearing men.

Reines was outspoken in his contention that Jewish education must be fostered in the traditional way. It must be upheld according to the scholars that possess the Halachic point of view and are fully aware of the cultural heritage and the supreme religious principles that must be inculcated in the youth.[46]

It must be noted that the reform movement in Germany had all the best intentions in mind when it began its new approach to re-educate the youth. However we are all aware of their shortcomings and failures because they sought to undermine the very essence of Judaism. Therefore, warns Reines, we must be extremely cautious when assuming a new venture in the scope of the educational system. Reines recalls the appalling scene of children entering the elementary school system completely ignorant of the basic tenets of the Jewish faith. Jews must be ever aware and cognizant of the abhorrent conditions that are prevalent in present day schools.[47]

Where is the yearning and love for the study of Torah? What has happened to our involvement in social problems in ameliorating the Jewish condition? The state of Russian Jewry is deplorable indeed. The sons of Zion are planting strange vineyards. They are ignoring Jewish tradition and have disregarded the traditional method of study. The Jewish people must assert themselves before the tide of assimilation becomes too great. Jews must be courageous in their effort and steadfast in their desire to study and dedicate their lives to the perpetuation of Halachic Judaism. The tragedy of Jewish youth is that they have no appreciation and a total lack of regard for the value and worthiness of the traditional literature. They are so removed from their literary fountain that they continually disregard it. Hence their appreciation and understanding becomes still further removed from the source of living truth.[48]

Would that the assimilated scholars understand that the Torah is based upon a logical order, with principles that are interconnected and interrelated. Then they would realize the greatness of the Torah. The oral law and more precisely the intricate sugyous or discourses on law, the homiletical and Midrashic passages have a certain nexus that binds them to-

---

[46] Isaac Jacob Reines, *Shnei Hamoros*, p. 7.
[47] Isaac Jacob Reines, *Chosem Tochnit*, p. 41.
[48] Isaac Jacob Reines, *Or Chodosh Al Zion*, p. 6.

gether. There is an everlasting and timeless unity that runs through the very core of the oral law. "Only you (the youth) are the leaders," Reines declared to the students of Yeshivath Etz Chaim. "Upon you is placed the onus and responsibility to guide and lead the future generation in the path of Torah and along the road of righteous and upright deeds." The Jewish people must be alerted to create a center of study for young men that will enable them to study in a more secure manner and thereby be capable of producing greater intellectual works. The Jewish people must always seek the greater productivity of their intellectual capabilities to foster and establish new citadels of culture that will be the bulwark to guard and defend the faith upon confrontation with all torment and turmoil so that they may be able to withstand the pressure and weather the peril. Only then shall the Jews prevail and maintain their identity with a timeless and everlasting quality.[49]

If the Israel community is to survive Jews must establish schools of high standards and of notable worth that will serve to restore the vigor and fortitude of the community in Israel. The Torah and culture for the new community is analogous to the soul in one's body. Therefore if Jews are to survive in Israel they must develop the soul, the spirit of the nation, a dynamic historical conception of the heritage. Jews must devote and dedicate their lives to the study of Torah with all its ramifications if they are to make their contribution to the continuity of Jewish history. The Jewish people must protect their Torah in face of all danger and must assert themselves no matter how grave the peril seems. The Bais Hamikdosh was created under fire from the enemy. The fortress of Yavneh was renewed amidst the terror and destruction that was cast upon it by the Romans. Confronting the enemy and overcoming the ensuing peril is the history of the Jew. In our time when Jews are faced with a terrible depression, both economic and cultural, Jews must guard themselves and maintain their heritage. It is incumbent upon them to assert themselves and be dedicated even more to the study of Torah.

---

[49] Isaac Jacob Reines, *Chosem Tochnit*, p. 4.

All those who abide by the oral law, namely those who cleave to its principles and precepts, have continued and maintained their identity. Those however who insist upon relying merely on the written law have failed miserably. The Bal Ha Turim notes quite poignantly the blessing "that an everlasting life you have planted amidst us" refers to the oral law. Only the oral law can be that vehicle which will transmit the vibrance and dynamism necessary to maintain and uphold the Jewish people in these trying times.[50]

The Jewish people are duty bound to take the light of the Torah from its case and expose it to their children so that they may be instructed and guided with the light of Torah. It is incumbent upon the Jewish people and moreover to make it known to their children and make them aware of the greatness of the Torah. As arrows in the hands of the mighty so is youth. Just as the arrow which is shot and cannot return because it must hit its mark, likewise it is with the years of youth. Man should divert and channel his energy and capacity toward the proper motivations and correct goals. He should use his ability to his ultimate capacity, for youth passes by like a falling star and after it has disappeared we can no longer recapture it. Therefore one should be diligent and not dispense his time in futile toil. Rather he should develop his faculties for educational purposes and stimulate his total being toward his cultural and spiritual development.

The Jewish civilization is a strong building. Although it has been decimated in many areas, the central core of the structure is ever-present and new stories will always be erected in this edifice with the tenets of faith and the principles that are transmitted in the oral law.[51]

Love of Torah is essential to the vitality of the Jewish community. Although a person may be merely a layman he can create for himself an everlasting existence in the conceptual scheme of the Jewish community. When he supports and seeks to be an economic benefactor to the scholar, his love of Torah contributes to the viability of the Jewish community. Although

---

[50] Isaac Jacob Reines, *Shnei Hamoros*, p. 34.
[51] *Ibid.*, p. 35.

a person learns but one chapter or even if he recites one sentence of the Torah, this spirit for the law transforms all his mundane acts into means that lead him towards his goal of being an upright person and a steadfast Jew. Hence the love for Torah per se is essential for the structure of Jewish education. One who has not appreciation and love for Torah will imagine and view the person who is inbred with the study of Torah as though he were erratic in his behavior and neurotic in his conduct. However, if one has a particular love for the Torah, he will necessarily be more likely to appreciate the people who study Torah.[52]

Although laymen are devoid of the knowledge that is required if one is to be a student and a scholar, nevertheless they can aspire to a high cultural plateau for although their ladder is set on the ground on a low plane nevertheless the top of the ladder can spiral to the heights of the sky. When one has an inexhaustible love for Torah he can transcend his meager knowledge with the emotional quality that is necessary for establishing a more perfect Judaism. They can reach a high level by virtue of their concern for the scholar and student.

The purpose of the Torah therefore is to reach out to all classes of Jews, not merely to be presented to the uniquely qualified man of genius capability, but also the Torah must extend itself to all persons encompassing various degrees of mental capability. This then is the purpose of the Torah. Love for Torah gives one a relationship with those who are not scholars. Although he may not be sufficiently equipped with the necessary knowledge of the Torah, nevertheless with his love for Torah he can ascend and aspire towards higher goals that will bring him nigh unto the Torah and thereby elevate his character to a higher spiritual plane.

When a man is immersed in his own daily activities he cannot direct his energy and time toward the study of Torah. If however his aim is motivated toward the proper goal of becoming elevated to G-d his intention is considered as though he had acted in accord with the highest spiritual motivation.

---

[52] *Ibid.*, p. 38.

"Set up for yourself signs and symbols," declares the prophet, "For when a person will embark upon a road toward returning to G-d he will have for himself a point of recognition where he can come back to G-d's worship." If a person sets up a sign, that means he has not discarded his original purpose completely and although he cannot now become preoccupied in the spiritual study of Torah, when he has the leisure time he will return because he has set up symbols in his mind to the effect that he has never forgotten the purpose of his life to be a student of the law and to be ultimately identified with the ideals of Torah.

When the Rabbis went to their work they told one another, "The stones of the sanctuary have been cast about." They were always aware of their spiritual devotion to G-d and although they were preoccupied in earning their livelihood they nevertheless had concern for the study of Torah. The sign that the holy stones of the sanctuary are being broken up is an expression of their lament for neglecting the study of Torah. Thus man can sublimate his mundane activities into a sublime religious experience if he is aware of his real goals in life and the immediate activities are transient in nature and only means to a higher spiritual end. Thus Midrash declares, "I will walk before G-d in the land of the living." Rabbi Judah commented that this sentence refers to a man who is preoccupied in the marketplace and is concerned with earning a livelihood. However, if he is constantly aware of his G-dliness, of his holiness, then the marketplace and all daily activities become transformed and sublimated into a higher and more important religious experience. All man's activities must be channeled and directed to higher goals and higher motivations. Therefore even the common man can aspire to reach the ultimate goal of cleaving unto G-d.[53]

The Torah states that it is a tree of life to all those who support and uphold it. Also the Torah states that cursed is he who does not uphold and fulfill the words of the Torah. The Torah is concerned and is interested primarily with its support

---

[53] Isaac Jacob Reines, *Chosem Tochnit*, p. 32, Isaac Jacob Reines, *Sefer Harochim*, p. 196.

and its fulfillment because if the Torah were to be concerned only with those who study it and those who are preoccupied and involved in the difficult discourses of the oral law, there would be few if any who would associate themselves with Judaism. Therefore the Torah states that it is a tree of life to those who support it even though they are not directly involved with it. Cursed is he who does not fulfill even though he does not study because the Torah is a practical way of life and the Torah is conscious of the fact that there are many people who are not equipped with sufficient capability of educating themselves. However they must endeavor to uphold and to fulfill its laws and obligations. This is the end result with which the Torah is primarily concerned and with this Jews must strive to be better Jews and improve their devotion to G-d.

To bestow pleasure upon the scholar and student is therefore the task of the laity. Therein can they maintain their identity with Judaism. The scholar is deemed with the same degree of sanctity as if he would be a scroll of the law. The talmid ehachem is considered to be like a *sefer* torah. As the Gemorah declares, "These are fools who rise before a Sefer Torah and who do not rise before the great scholar." Cleaving and identifying oneself with the scholar is a manner of associating with the ultimate ideals of Judaism. As the Rabbis conveyed this idea in the passage written in the Torah, "And you who cleave unto G-d have an everlasting life." How can one cleave unto G-d? He is but a consuming fire. However, he who associates himself with scholars and saints of Judaism has fulfilled his obligation of becoming identified with the Torah and G-d. Thus supporting and appreciating the scholar is the means for the laity of clinging and identifying themselves with the centrality of Judaism. And you shall search in the afternoon as the blind person searches at night. What difference does it make to the blind person if he searches in the darkness, in the night or if he searches in the daytime. Rabbi Jose declares that the blind person if he has a torch to guide him, will make people aware that he is disabled and they will come to his assistance. Hence it is also with the study of Torah. Even if a person is remotely removed from its study yet if he associates himself with those who study and he aspires to relate himself with the scholars then his life assumes the light of Torah and his spirit becomes illuminated with the glow of the scholar.[54]

The term, children of the flock, that we pray on the high holy days is indicative of the laity who strive and aspire to be led by the scholars and students. If the laymen involve themselves in prayer and associate with the scholar in an effort to help the latter, to give him economic support and other means of sustenance, then they will pass through the Judgment Day and like flock will be elevated by their pastor.[55]

The Jewish people should not only be concerned with the maintenance of the scholar, but also must acquire the best books so that the scholar may broaden his concepts and sharpen his perception of the Torah. Hence through the acquisition of books, Jews establish a strong scholarly foundation wherein the scholar has a base to create and develop new principles and new theories in Halacha. What is the treasure that a man can assemble in his home and what is the everlasting charity? It is if one lends out his books, his Tanach, Talmud and other sacred books that the scholar may be able to study them assiduously and involve himself in the learning process. How are women privileged with a great deal of security? What is the everlasting quality that is characteristic of their blissful welfare? "Because," answers Rabbi Chiya, "They watch their children until their husbands return from study and prayer, they are concerned with the rearing of their children—that their children should have the nurturing of spiritual development." Women take care of the children when their husbands are away. Hence women are indispensable to the spiritual and cultural development of their children. If it is believed that the Torah is divine, that it has been disseminated from Heaven, then it can be readily understood why the Torah has an everlasting quality. The two are interwoven and intertwined. Everything which is spiritual in nature is timeless in quality. Therefore the Torah is infinite in its continuity, everlasting.[56]

---

[54] Isaac Jacob Reines, *Sefer Harochim*, p. 198.
[55] Isaac Jacob Reines, *Chosem Tochnit*, p. 34.
[56] Isaac Jacob Reines, *Sefer Herochim*, pp. 169-171.

G-d and all His Appellations are placed in the ark because the Torah represents G-d and the entire Torah is the expression of G-d. Hence everything that is written in the Torah can be called the appellation of G-d. Therefore when the Torah is placed in the ark, G-d's name and everything pertaining to G-d is also in the ark because the Torah is the representative of G-d. It is the expression of G-d. Natural phenomena are but simile and metaphor for spiritual reflection and comprehension. Thus Reines infers from the blessing—*yotzar* or—a reflection of the light of Torah. If G-d is thanked for natural light then it is only logical to extend that appreciation for the light and illumination of Torah. The slumberer dreams and his thoughts do not adjust to reality and likewise all his thoughts that are not in the scope of the conception of Torah are incongruous and unrealistic. Hence only thought within the guidelines of Torah is the practical way wherein one can lead a fruitful spiritual life. The Torah is the spirit and lifeline of Israel. One who disparages and belittles the Torah is likened to one who sheds blood. The Talmud relates a story of Titus who defiled and blasphemed the Sanctuary. When he was in the process of his vicious act the cover of the ark dripped with blood to demonstrate that whoever desecrates the Sanctuary of Israel is wounding its soul and is damaging the essence of Judaism. When the mountain of Sinai was lifted like a barrel to destroy Israel the Jews experienced the Torah on that momentous occasion and if they would have not received the Torah they would have inevitably felt that they were not worthy to live. For as Reines believes, only with the Torah can one really be qualified to assume the title of man. Hence there wouldn't be any legitimate reason for living if they hadn't accepted the Torah with all its ramifications.[57]

Don't call it My Sanctuary but read it My sanctifiers because the holiness of G-d is represented by its scholars and saints. The Torah raises the national pride of the Jewish people. It inspires Jews with the courage and conviction to continue and carry on with the process of learning and pattern of study. The first

---

[57] Isaac Jacob Reines, *Chosem Tochnit*, p. 37.

blessing of the Torah declares this very fact. It says, "You, O G-d, have chosen us and given us the Torah." Jews are chosen only for their involvement in Torah and commitment to its teachings. Reines concludes that the youth should be commended when they undertake the study of Torah and should be exposed to the proper pride of their people. That is, if one reveres the Torah he reveres the national pride of the Jewish heritage. This is the correct pride that should be sought—not false pride, but a sense of dignity and a reverence for a higher spiritual goal. Hence the pride of the people and the law are interrelated. The pride of Israel cannot be severed from its love for the Torah and appreciation of its teachings. The houses of study and prayer have an immeasurable quality and convey a source of dignity for the nation. Indeed there is a dispute as to which is the greater source of sanctity—the house of Torah or the house of worship. However, the place where one studies Torah must also be consecrated and is also a holy location. Hence this gives rise to a more spiritual study, for if the place where study takes place has so high a degree of sanctity then of course what will be studied will convey the spiritual lesson and sublime study of the Torah.

Involvement in the study of Torah removes all types of pain and one becomes insensitive to his suffering because the pleasure that one derives from the study of Torah uplifts the soul and transforms the personality in the direction of happiness. The spirit of Torah and the emotional quality of Torah inspire one to overcome his problems and to sidestep the many obstacles that confront him. The righteous person who studies the Torah demonstrates that the Divine walks with him wherever he goes. Thus the Zaddik, the righteous man, is symbolic of the Shechina, divine inspiration, and whatever the Zaddik creates is a reflection of the glory and beauty of G-d. As Rabbi Simon Bar Yochai observed, wherever the Zaddikim go the Shechina is reflected in their presence. Those who disregard the glory of the Torah will be consumed as Isaiah prophesied. The Talmud comments that if one leaves the synagogue when the Sefer Torah is being read he will be consumed because he demonstrates his lack of concern and complete abhorrence for the study of Torah which is the centrality and the very core of Judaism. The Torah is an internal nexus between man and his fellow man. Although a person may depart for a particular venture the moral bond that a man makes with his friend on an intellectual level will be permanent and everlasting in his memory. The Torah is that vehicle which leads to everlasting friendship. As the Rabbis stated, "He who departs from his fellow should not leave him without discussing some problem in the law because it symbolizes the eternal friendship that is drawn from the well of intellectual association." However, one who is merely associated with his friend in a natural and pleasant way has formed a relationship which is only temporary in essence and will not survive for a long while. The intellectual bond is one which is imbued with love and it is through this that man loves his fellow man. It is noteworthy that the Torah characterizes the love relationship of man and his wife with the term *vayeda,* meaning that he lived with her because the intellectual person has the supreme love for his fellow man. Ideas supersede all sorts of prejudices and the person who is imbued with only the intellectual approach to life will always love his fellow man. The leaders of Israel and those who interpret the law are the very essence of Israel's survival. Without a tradition of customs and laws Israel could not maintain its historical identity in the face of all danger and throughout such travail.[58]

The great man or the leader in Israel deposits his attributes into the historical memorial of future generations. His deeds are recorded as a model and lesson for coming generations. The way he overcomes seemingly insurmountable obstacles is through a shining example for future time. The Torah is like a shield before the sword because the idea of the sword is corrosive and destructive. The sword symbolizes man's brutality and inhumanity towards his fellow man. All material lusts are symbolized with the passion of the sword and man's drive toward annihilating his fellow man for his own personal gain is characterized by it. Only the Torah, the Sefer, the Book, the Scroll can be

---

[58] Isaac Jacob Reines, *Shnei Hamoros,* p. 8.

a shield and protector against man's inhumanity to his fellow man. The Torah gives man the emotional fervor that is denied to him when he pursues the passion of his material exploits. The Torah is the ammunition that delivers him from the disruptive and degradating descent to the abyss that is characterized by man's pursuit of absolute pleasure.[59]

The Torah has been the armor which has shielded the Jews throughout the great titanic waves of history. Israel was not swept away by the storm and fury of the assimilating tide like other nations. Rather she has held her head high above the stormy sea of assimilation. The Torah is the *raison d'être* of the Jewish people. It alone is the coat of armor that protects Jews in battle. Therefore the Rabbis declared: "Gird your sword, don't be afraid, you hero." The Rabbis expressed this verse in Psalms to refer to the scholar who should always be alert and on guard, for life is an everlasting battle.[60]

The laws of the Torah are reflected in nature. When we observe the ocean trying to flood the beachhead we experience a lesson in Jewish History. Throughout Jewish peril and travail the nations of the world endeavored to annihilate and to dissolve Judaism. The Torah has been the beachhead from which are launched Jewish cultural goals and social aims. It has stood the test of time and like the beach will never be flooded. The nations of the world can never sweep away the current of Judaic culture. The beach is timeless but the tide merely temporal. On the beaches of the earth where the enemy seeks to scuttle Jewish survival it is necessary to establish the bulwark of Judaism. "I am as a fortress and my breasts are like towers," says Solomon in Canticles. "I am like a wall," declared the Rabbis. The "I" refers to the scholars and to the people as a whole. And the towers of Jewish strength are the Torah and the places, the sanctuaries where Torah is studied. Jewish fortresses are erected with spiritual strength and the towers are the lookouts and watchplaces where Jews can nurture and develop this spirit. This is why Jews have survived, for only with spirit of Torah

---

[59] *Ibid.*, p. 9.
[60] Isaac Jacob Reines, *Orim Gerolim*, p. 92.

can Jews override the great abuse and destruction that has been heaped against their fortress. The foundation however has not been rocked and the fortress of Judaism stands ever guarded and ever alert.[61]

The Torah is not merely a watchtower or a fortress where Jews preserve their principles and keep a steady vigilance that will not be submerged in the sea of assimilation. Rather it has been a contributing force to all the nations of the world. Jews have infused and injected the Gentile world with their dynamism, with their vibrance for living. When the nations of the world observe that the Jew risks his life, all the material wealth that he has gathered for the sake of the Torah, for the sake of the spirit, then and only then will they realize that with their spirit of dedication to the study of the Torah Jews are not only defending their faith but are also demonstrating that the life of Torah will prevail over the life of futile materialism.[62]

The nationalism of the Jew is dependent upon his Torah study. Without Torah, without mitzvohs, without commandments the Jewish nation has no viability, no life. Hence the Torah is the spinal cord of nationalism and the centrality of its growth. The beauty of the Torah and its majestic charm are expressed when one immerses himself completely in its study. When one studies the laws concerning a particular commandment the Torah considers it as if the student had fulfilled the obligation of the mitzvoh. When one studies the laws concerning sacrifices in the Temple, the Torah considers it as if he would have sacrificed upon the altar. The greatness of the Torah consists in the fact that it gives life to all those who abide by it and study it. The Torah gives life because it knows no social distinctions and does not recognize any aristocracy. All persons are equal in the study of the law as it is written in *Avoth*—Be aware of the children who come from poor people for from them shall rise Torah. It is an aristocracy of knowledge.[63]

The Torah does not conceal itself and is not afraid of being revealed for all who seek the truth and desire to explore and

---

[61] Isaac Jacob Reines, *Orah V'Simchah*, p. 84.
[62] Isaac Jacob Reines, *Or Chodosh Al Zion*, p. 71.
[63] Isaac Jacob Reines, *Chosem Tochnit*, p. 45.

uncover its real essence. For truth can be exposed for all to observe and to investigate it. However, people who seek to lie, conceal their steps and disguise their ideology lest someone may trace the hidden meaning and reveal their naked shame. The Torah is the Book of Life and the Book of Truth, open for all to scrutinize and to examine closely. The Rabbis declared that whoever studies alone and isolates and segregates himself shall be consumed by the sword because the Torah must be open to all and its goal and purpose is to enhance Judaism by expressing and declaring its principles and ideals in a clarion call so all may hear, all may listen.[64]

The Torah was given in five thundering voices, and a great trumpet was heard to announce the reception of the Torah because the veracity of the Torah is not to be held in seclusion but rather must be proclaimed to all. If Jews demonstrate their zeal for expressing the Torah to the multitudes, then they fulfill His command, and are G-d's servants. The *tefillin* shall be unto you as a symbol. The Rabbis declared that the *tefillin shel yod,* the *tefillin* that one places on his hand should be concealed. However the *tefillin* that one places on his head should be revealed for all. "The idea," says Reines, "is to express and convey the notion that the *tefillin* of the hand represent action, certain *maasim,* certain deeds that a person does. These should be concealed, for a man should have humility before G-d and not be an exhibitionist. However, the *tefillin* that represent the head are an expression of one's thought. It is open for all to criticize and to examine." Therefore the *tefillin* symbolizing man's thought, man's comprehension of ideas should be disclosed to all.

Knowledge and understanding recognize no boundaries. You cannot suppress knowledge, for knowledge cries out and wisdom proclaims its voice. One's quest for Torah is similar to one's drive to replenish his physical needs. Therefore the Torah is equated and analogized to water. The Rabbis declare that water refers to Torah. Man has to quench his spiritual thirst, his spiritual drive in the same manner that he seeks to refresh

---

[64] Isaac Jacob Reines, *Eduth B'Yaacov,* p. 24.

himself when he is thirsty. The Torah has also been equated to fire. Man's complete involvement with burning energy necessitates him to involve himself creatively in the study of Torah. Now water is natural. It flows. However, fire must be created. These are the two categories, two modes of study that are equivalent to the elements of water and fire.[65]

The Torah is the dew that gives rise to and restores man's glory. It is the resurrection of man's spirit. Although the Jew may seem to disintegrate and disappear, almost miraculously he rises and rejuvenates himself because of the spark and spirit of the Torah. The wisdom of the Torah reflects itself upon man's face. When a person studies the Torah his entire countenance shines with its radiance. The Torah gives man a certain luster to electrify his personality.[66]

The Torah is the reservoir where man can draw upon all his material needs and psychic drives. It is the source from which man can derive his spiritual satisfaction to replenish his soul, for all the laws and decrees of the Torah were governed and declared to man that he may live by them, that man shall actively fulfill them. The Torah also says that you are called man because the laws, principles and ethical system that is inherent within it makes him cognizant of his humanity.[67]

What gives the Jew the tenacity to cling to his faith? It is that he is classified as a Jew by his name. A Jew even if he sins and violates the law is still considered a Jew because we see in our time that although the Jews are persecuted and afflicted in many ways and even though they turn from the righteous path and transgress, they nevertheless maintain their Jewish identity and cling to their historical commitment.

Let us consider the entire Jewish culture with which the Jew should associate and to which he should cleave. How rich and fruitful are the Torah and mitzvohs, all precepts and commandments. If one abides by them, his whole life is permeated by their sanctity. If that is the case then the Jewish will be

---

[65] Isaac Jacob Reines, *Chosem Tochnit*, p. 48.
[66] Isaac Jacob Reines, *Sefer Harochim*, pp. 261-263.
[67] Isaac Jacob Reines, *Orah V'Simchah*, p. 41.

assured of their continuity and secure in their mission to advance the cause of Judaism.[68]

"There is no section in the Torah from which we cannot infer the resurrection of the dead," declares Rabbi Simoi. The Torah is the supreme source of sustenance. Every sentence of the Torah is replete and overflowing with the cognizance of resurrection and rejuvenation. The emotional spark is ignited throughout the entire Torah and everywhere we look we can find our source of redemption and the spark of resurrection.[69]

The rainbow did not appear during the lifetime of Rabbi Shimon Bar Yochai because his spiritual glow and his cultural influence which was diffused among the entire population of Israel was sufficient so that no miracle was necessary, no rainbow to demonstrate G-d's majesty was required. It was Rabbi Shimon, the Son of Jochai, who created a flowing spiritual continuum where the glowing and sparkling Torah was ever present and ever prevalent for all Jewry. Even the laity were imbued with the sanctity of the Torah and the light of his personality permeated within every person and his brilliance shone throughout the entire world.[70]

The yoke of Sennecherib was broken by the oil that was poured and anointed on the neck of every Jew by Hezekiah the King. Hezekiah lit the light of Torah mitzvohs and precepts throughout the entire community of Israel. Everywhere Torah was studied from Dan to Beersheba. No one was found to be ignorant of the laws of purity and contamination. Everyone was literate. Thus the intellectual ointment of the Torah soothed the burdening yoke of Sennecherib and softened the marks of his yoke until the rope of the oppressor was snapped and the Jewish people asserted their individuality and independence. The Torah was given in the month of Sivan, and was characterized with luster and glamor. It is called the month of Ziv. It is no mere coincidence that the Torah was given in the month of beauty and adornment. It indicates that the Torah

---

[68] Isaac Jacob Reines, *Sefer Harochim*, p. 198.
[69] Isaac Jacob Reines, *Or Chodosh Al Zion*, p. 94.
[70] Isaac Jacob Reines, *Or Shivat Ha-Yomim*, p. 44.

is adorned with beauty and gives luster to those who abide by its laws and study its precepts.[71]

Everyone agrees, declares the Talmud, that on *Shevuoth* or as it is called in the Talmud—*atzeret*—a person should enjoy himself not only spiritually but also that he should satiate his physical needs—eating, drinking, merrymaking, because the Torah recognizes man's needs. It does not tell man to abandon his pleasures, his physical drives. Rather the Torah insists upon sublimating them and transforming one's character to a higher spiritual plane and elevating oneself unto G-d. "And you should love G-d with both your inclinations, not only with good inclinations but also with the evil one," declared the Rabbis. To serve G-d, man needs all his faculties and he must transform his personality not to be seduced by it nor to isolate himself from the community. In fact, the Rabbis declared that he who vows to become a Nazarite is considered to be a sinner because Judaism recognizes that man must take an active participating role in life and not to segregate himself from the community at large. The Rabbis were cognizant of man's psychic drives and all the inclinations which make up the human personality. They stated in many places that it is a *chazoko* that man does not engage in intercourse which is licentious in nature. Or they maintained that it is an established axiom that a person has a certain innate quality of dignity which normally tends to give him a reputable character. They also had many other established axioms concerning monetary laws, as for example a person will not despise his fellow man in a legal quarrel. The Torah was not given to the angels. It was intended for man. That is it was created to serve man and to elevate him unto G-d. All man's drives are to be sublimated by the supreme value of the Torah. The Torah was intended to uplift man and to elevate his character. It was given for him, that he might ascend and aspire toward the ideal of G-dliness.

There are two categories of servitude by which man is bound. There is a natural type of employment, for example, a son serving his father. There is also a compulsory form of em-

---

[71] Isaac Jacob Reines, *Sefer Harochim*, p. 221.

ployment—a servant serving his master. The son serves because of love and has a supreme desire to fulfill the commandment to honor his parents while the servant works because of necessity and fear. The latter has no real appreciation for his master. Likewise the Torah represents the servitude of a son to his parents. It represents the natural love of man to G-d. It is the expression of man's devotion and subordination to G-d because of love and sincere desire to emulate G-d's ways. The material world is equivalent to the servant who must work at menial tasks for his master. It is not his natural love but rather one that is borne with great toil and misery. This is what the Rabbis meant when they declared that he who involves himself in the study of Torah removes from his path the burden and yoke of governmental laws and economic problems. When Jews serve G-d and are devoted to His Torah they are called Sons of G-d. If however, they do not serve G-d they are called His slaves. The Rabbis were keenly aware of the two-fold relationship of man's service to G-d—the natural one and the compulsory one. The Torah fosters within man a natural love for G-d and stimulates within him the desire to serve G-d with all his love, not from fear as is the relationship of the servant to his master. This is the supreme function of the Torah, that is, to encourage us to be G-d's children and not His slaves.[72]

The Torah is encased and encircled in roses. The strength of the Torah does not lie in the fact that it needs external fortresses, i.e., external blockades to protect it. Rather it alone is the fortress and is encircled in roses, in the beauty of its fragrance and in the adornment of its esthetic nature. This is the Torah's defense mechanism. The Torah does not need external forms of protection. The Torah itself is internally created to reinforce lives and strengthen souls. It alone is the source of survival.[73]

He who is involved and completely dedicated to the spirit of its study is called a free man. As the Rabbis declare in *The Ethics of the Fathers*: We have three classes of people namely

---

[72] Isaac Jacob Reines, *Sharay Orah,* p. 26.
[73] Isaac Jacob Reines, *Or Shivat Ha-Yomim,* p. 48.

the righteous, the wicked and those who are in between. The latter's status is difficult to ascertain. The righteous person is ruled and regulated by his good inclinations. The evil person on the other hand is overpowered by his evil inclinations. The man in the middle lives in conflict with the perplexing problems which engulf his life. The manner in which a person can extricate himself from the plight of his peril and his problems is to resolve his situation and live within the scope of his good inclinations. If he will always be immersed in Torah study, only then will he overcome his immediate environment. Therein the Rabbis declared can the person be called truly free. One does not escape from freedom but rather freedom is a way of life.[74]

He who is immersed in the study of Torah will have the burden and yoke of governmental regulations and economic problems removed from him by G-d. Both are means to eradicate the evil in man. That is, Torah strives to uplift man. However, the Torah way of living is internal and inspires emotional fervor for the religious ideal. The economic and governmental method of developing man's behavior and his attitude toward a normal way of living is external. It does not develop man's spiritual genius. It is rather external in nature. Therefore the Rabbis were keenly aware to denote that Torah supersedes material goals of establishing one's self in society. The Torah is the primary force of man's establishment in society. His roots are created in culture and not in material splendor nor are they created by governmental organization. They are but external features that can only supplement the Torah.[75]

The way of the righteous is however difficult at first. The Rabbis were keenly aware of this. They noted that the way of the righteous is painful and painstaking at first. However, it is blissful and enriching when the person reaches his spiritual plateau. He must assert himself and involve himself completely in spiritual ideas. Only then will he reap the fruits of his labor.[76]

What is the profit if man toils? "There is no profit in man's toil except if he immerses himself in the study of Torah," de-

---

[74] Isaac Jacob Reines, *Sefer Harochim*, p. 263.
[75] Isaac Jacob Reines, *Chosem Tochnit*, p. 49.
[76] Isaac Jacob Reines, *Sefer Harochim*, p. 263.

clares the Midrash. Only his toil in Torah can develop and serve as a source of continuity. All other aspects of his labor are futile because they do not develop the soul and don't give expression for spiritual attainment and self-perfection.[77]

The goal of the Torah is to give man spiritual development and cultural advancement. He must always progress and continually strive to attain perfection. The Rabbis were keenly aware of this and expressed this idea within the context of the phrase—And you shall observe My law. He who has observed the law and has studied it has attained his essence and created himself. He has developed himself into a spiritual being. What is the distinction between the animal and man? The Midrash comments that an ox or a sheep or a lamb remains as it has been born. Man however is involved in a constant development, in a daily progression and his life is never ending. It continues for future generations. He has to rear children and grandchildren who will be immersed in the study of Torah and dedicated to all its principles. The animal on the other hand doesn't need any spiritual attainment. Its life is based on its physical growth and decay. Man however can never withdraw to such a state of being. His divine spark drives him to attain spiritual perfection. It is his categorical imperative. This is the distinction between man and animal. Man has a spiritual need to elevate himself and to transform his being into that of a G-d-fearing individual.[78]

How can we discern the man who has attained perfection from the one who is lowly and debased in his spiritual endeavor? It is only through the development of his soul and his cultural fulfillment. This development is expressed and demonstrated only by his fulfillment of his Torah study and in his observance of the mitzvohs. The generation is viewed also within this context. If the generation has excelled then it has developed through Torah mitzvohs. If the generation is degenerate in nature then we can only attest that it has not developed itself spiritually. The source of progress is spiritual development.

---

[77] Isaac Jacob Reines, *Orah V'Simchah*, p. 74.
[78] Isaac Jacob Reines, *Or Chodosh Al Zion*, p. 59.

If man has developed himself with all his potential in all his spiritual endeavors, then his development has been realized. This is the expression of his total being. If a man is degenerate it is only because he has not sought to develop himself and to seek his spiritual expression within his personality. Progress is contingent upon spiritual development for they are intertwined.[79]

The purpose of creation is to produce the man who has attained spiritual perfection. As the Rabbis comment, "The Torah itself declared to man that the purpose of the Torah is to develop the human qualities within man." The person who recognizes the humanitarian qualities that are inherent within the human being becomes ever closer to G-d. Thus we note that Abraham recognized his Creator because he was cognizant of his fellow man. This is the purpose of the Torah, namely to imbue man with the desire to excel and to attain his goal of ultimate commitment to G-d.[80]

"The Torah drains man's energy," declares the Rabbis. This is to symbolize that man is not made or created to exert his power. He cannot live by his might. Rather he can only prevail if his potential and energetic capacity is diverted and channeled toward the study of Torah. Torah superimposes upon man the right of intellect. It is the Torah that must prevail and not might.[81]

Torah and mitzvohs were given to purify man and to sublimate his personality and to transcend his being so that he may become nigh unto G-d. The Rabbis comment, "You shall love your neighbor as yourself." "This is the greatest principle in the Torah," declares Rabbi Akiba. All the precepts of the Torah lead toward one goal, that of understanding one's fellow man to the degree that one loves his own person. The purpose of the Torah is to inculcate man with the ethical ideals and the moral principles to the degree that it becomes natural to him. The *musar*, the ethical, becomes *teva*, routinized nature.[82]

---

[79] *Ibid.*, p. 60.
[80] Isaac Jacob Reines, *Sefer Harochim*, p. 240.
[81] *Ibid.*, p. 241.

Every person is commanded to write his own scroll of the law. He must develop his own Torah within his personality. Every person develops according to his own potential and mental capacity. Therefore he alone must be the writer of his destiny. He must record his deeds and acts with which he involves himself and in which he participates in his daily activity. This is inherent within the concept that every man must write his own scroll. "Write them on the tablets of your heart," declare the Proverbs. The Torah then must become inscribed in one's heart.[83]

In reciting the blessing on the Torah before actually reading it we say, "Blessed are you, O G-d, who has chosen us from all nations." After reading the Torah Jews declare, "Blessed are you, O G-d, who has given us the Torah way of life, the true way of living." Why do Jews say before the reading—that you have given us? Reines suggests that this is comparable to other blessings which are pronounced concerning pleasure that is derived. For example, if one eats bread, first he blesses G-d who has created the bread and afterwards when he has completed his meal he blesses G-d for the pleasure that he has derived from that particular meal. Hence also with regard to the law, Jews first bless G-d who is the cause of the blessing, who is the One who has provided Jews with the means to become spiritually elevated unto Him. Then they bless G-d for the benefit which they have derived.

We have endeavored to summarize herein the basic ideas that Reines has developed within his educational system and intellectual guide for man's personal development. According to Reines, the Torah which is the centrality of Jewish development must always be perpetuated, continued and developed. The Torah is not a static group of laws. It is a dynamic system of abstract concepts that are creative in nature and productive in scope. The function then of the educational system is to inspire Jews with its ever-present vitality and ever-growing dynamism.

---

[83] *Ibid.*, p. 242.

# 4

# Ideas on Zionism

The Torah has delivered a covenant to Israel. The words of the oath of the covenant are a remarkable portrayal of the Jewish historic destiny. Throughout the Jewish travail in exile and throughout its historic torment and turbulent times Jews have experienced an unusual phenomena that is unique. Jews have maintained their identity amidst all conflict and have prevailed to uphold their national spirit. This is a sign that G-d has proclaimed to Israel what with all its suffering and with all the burdening misery it will experience nevertheless it will retain its name. "And I will destroy your sanctuary," declared the Rabbis. Although it is destroyed it is continually called sanctuary. Every nation has realized the unusual phenomena that in Israel although the Jewish people have been removed from their territory the land has never been rebuilt.

It is an axiom that the Jewish religion and nation are inextricably intertwined as we have explained in the section on the biography of Reines. It is an unusual phenomena that such a nation has maintained and survived without a national homeland, without any territory. It is because Jews have always strived and hoped to survive without a national homeland, without any territory. It is because Jews have always strived and hoped to experience a return to their promised land that the emotional drive has ignited their spirit and sparked their hope to exist throughout these millennium of misfortune. Only the Jewish nation has preserved its sense of nationality because it has kept within it the burning hope and everlasting desire to once again recapture its homeland. The firm belief is that Jews will return for if they have no belief in their return then their whole religion is without foundation. Belief in Israel is intricably intertwined with the Jewish religion.[1]

A voice declares in the desert, "Clear the road for my people to re-enter their promised land." The prophet was aware of the fact that when the Jewish people are removed from their territory, the land becomes a desert. The land cannot be plowed and the soil cannot be tilled without the Jewish people as its inhabitants. The prophet therefore uses the term, calling in the wilderness, in the desert, because so long as Israel is not on the soil of its homeland then Israel remains a desert. When Jews are in exile, the land is also in exile for the land of Israel suffers alongside its people and the pain of her people is felt by the soil. The land of Israel which is the city of G-d contains the personality of its nation.[2]

The link between the Jewish people and its land is an unusual and unique phenomenon. It is difficult to explain and is far removed from comprehension. After the assurance that the land of Israel will always exist the Torah concludes in the portion of *Nedarim* with the phrase: The secrets belong to G-d and those which are revealed belong to our children. The secret of the Jewish survival and the anomaly that the state of Israel has remained barren and desolate for so many millennium is difficult to ascertain and hard to comprehend. Nevertheless it is a fact that Israel and its land shall survive in the face of all peril.

When G-d confronts Moses in the scene of the burning bush, Moses observes that the bush burns and is consumed and still remains in its essence. The bush shall never perish. So is it with Israel and her land. Although they are torn asunder and persecution engulfs their very existence, nevertheless they will maintain their identity throughout the travail that they have experienced and endured.[3]

The land of Israel can only contain those who are spiritually

---

[1] Isaac Jacob Reines, *Chosem Tochnit*, p. 54
[2] Isaac Jacob Reines, *Or Chodosh Al Zion*, p. 114.
[3] Isaac Jacob Reines, *Orah V'Simchah*, p. 94.

qualified to enjoy it. "And the land shall not expel you," declares Scripture. "For when a man eats food which does not agree with him he vomits it." Israel's land is very similar and analogous to man's food. If Jews are spiritually deserving of Israel then they have the right to settle there.

The Rabbis point out that the land is like a deer. The skin of a live deer is taut and once the skin is removed it cannot be replaced on the deer. The land of Israel is also similar to this. If the people are culturally imbued with the principles of its religion then it can contain all the Jews. However, when the Jewish people renounce their religion and cast aside the very principles that have been transmitted to them throughout the ages, then Israel is like the dead deer upon whom you cannot replace the stripped skin. Therefore Jews have to seek and strive to elevate themselves to that spiritual plane that will enable them to resettle and revitalize the land.[4]

There is an internal relationship between the land of Israel and its people. G-d measured all the land in the earth and declared that Israel belonged to the Jewish people. Many precepts and commandments are reserved specifically to be performed only in Israel. As the Jewish people are commanded to observe the Sabbath, similarly Israel has its Sabbath when the land cannot be tilled and the soil cannot be plowed. There is a spiritual tie and cultural link between Israel and its people like that of body and soul; therefore the mission of Israel on its land is to be experienced only there. The cultural mission is to be exercised only there. No other territory is suited for this spiritual task. The purpose of the Jewish people is to fulfill its mission on its own soil.

The Uganda project could not have survived. It was only a temporary measure. It is also known that Reines, who was agreeable to the Uganda solution, stated quite succinctly to Zangwill that it would only be a temporary and brief interlude. Israel must, Reines declared, experience her spiritual destiny on the promised land which was sworn to her forefathers.[5]

---

[4] *Ibid.*, p. 95.
[5] Isaac Jacob Reines, *Sefer Harochim*, p. 147.

When Abraham saw that in Israel the people plow and prune in the proper time, that they are diligent and industrious in their labor and agricultural productivity, he declared that this is the land that he would desire for his descendants. Only a land that can inspire and invigorate its inhabitants is the promised land that the Jewish people shall possess. This was the dream of Abraham that the Jewish people should inherit a land that can imbue them with a feeling for work: A land that can extract our sweat, the sweat of our brow. This was Abraham's wish. Jews do not need a land that will make them idle or delinquent. Jews need a land that will evoke the response of labor and toil. Israel expresses that hope. There is an emotional attachment beween the land and its people as may be demonstrated by the Calutzim. Jews take pride in Israel and Israel takes pride in the Jews. This is the bond that ties the Jews to the land, inspiring them with the drive and energy to fulfill their spiritual goals and cultural tasks. It is the motivational force and spiritual source of their intellectual and creative dreams to enhance their culture and to contribute also to civilization in general.[6]

The month of Nissan is the first month in the Jewish calendar. The Torah should have started with this very sentence. Why does it begin with the history of world civilization up to emergence of the Jewish people? This question was raised by Rabbi Yitzchak and quoted in the first Rashi on Genesis. He answers that the Torah wanted to convey the idea that the entire world belongs to G-d and whatever G-d desires to bequeath to a particular nation, He does so with His will; and that the Jewish people are not robbers, and did not capture the land with their own audacity as one may suppose. Rather it is because of G-d's will that they captured Israel. It is G-d's desire that the Jewish people take the land away from the Canaanites and resettle it.

What is the nexus between the precept of enumerating the months and the story of Creation? Counting the months and the entire system of astronomical galaxies is a unique science.

---

[6] Werfel, *op. cit.*, p. 364.

As the Talmud declares: For this is your wisdom and scholarship to demonstrate before the nations of the world. It is the talent and knowledge of being able to ascertain the calendar and the understanding of the entire celestial system. All this is based upon intellectual human skill. It is rooted in a capability to grasp the fundamental laws of natural science. History, however, which is the story of *Genesis* up to that particular sentence in the portion of *Bo,* expresses the idea of *emunah.* Therefore the story of *Bereshit* demonstrates that we cannot rely purely upon intellectual acumen. Jews must be endowed with a high degree of spiritual belief in G-d. Only if their speculation is predicated upon belief in G-d can it have an everlasting content. Therefore Rabbi Yitzchak wanted to express the idea that if Jews have the belief that everything belongs to G-d, then the claim of the Gentiles that they have stolen Israel from them is ludicrous for it is G-d's world, and to whom G-d wishes He shall bequeath that land. If Jews have the belief then they can assure themselves that Israel will attest to the survival of the Jewish people. Insofar as the Jewish people resettle Israel, so they become everlasting.[7]

If one assimilates on the foreign soil where he has settled, then it is a true sign that he wishes to relinquish his ties, his historical bond with the promised land. However the Jewish people have never assimilated with the foreign culture. They have merely adopted some external features or aspects of the foreign civilization. Internally, however, Jews retain their identity and aspire for the return to their homeland.

There are two categories of possession that man has. One is the natural possession, the other is the ethical one. When a man buys an object from his friend he has the physical right of ownership and also the ethical one. Similarly with the land of Israel Jews have an ethical tie for G-d has given them this land. G-d doesn't say that I will give, rather He declares that He has given it to the Jews, to the descendants of Abraham, Isaac and Jacob. Therefore they have the ethical assurance that Israel belongs to them. However they lack the natural assurance

---

[7] Isaac Jacob Reines, *Orah V'Simchah,* p. 88.

that is, they do not have physical access to Israel. (This of course was in Reines' time.) Therefore we hope and pray to G-d that all Israel will not only be ethically assured to the Jews but also that they should have the natural possession of Israel, the right of access, the right to build and to establish the Jewish society on its soil.

When one inherits a personal possession, he guards, maintains and preserves it. He strives with all his emotional capacity and endeavors to guard it. He endears and cherishes it. How much more so shall the Jews strive to uphold, maintain and preserve their homeland in Israel. It is the homeland of all Jewry. It is the territory, the inheritance of every Jew. It is not merely a personal possession but the possession of the total Jewish community. It is shared by all and everyone has an equal opportunity for its rich inheritance. When we see how much blood has been shed throughout the ages, how much travail has been endured for maintaining the idea of Israel, Jews should assert themselves and be filled with emotion. Their hearts should be uplifted with the desire to rebuild their homeland, the birthplace of their forefathers.

The sin of the spies, contends Reines, was a result of their lack of emotional attachment to Israel. They were not able to evaluate Israel properly. Hence they were gripped by fear and engulfed with terror of the giants that were observed in Israel. They did not have the belief that the land of Israel is intertwined with the people. They were not able to associate themselves with Israel because they permitted fear to overwhelm them. They should have been immersed with the spirit, the *regesh* of Israel.[8]

Israel is distinguished from the Diaspora by two characteristics. In the first place the land of Israel is endowed with a specific degree of sanctity that is above and beyond all other lands. It has the sanctity of its settlers, that is its settlers create a sanctity within the land. There are many precepts which can only be observed in Israel. These are the precepts that relate to the soil as for example tithing, the jubilee and the sabbatical

---

[8] Isaac Jacob Reines, *Or Chodosh Al Zion*, p. 184.

year. The land as we have seen previously contains a Kedusha. G-d has bequeathed it to the community of Israel. Jews have been assured that this land is theirs. It has been promised to them. However a land without settlers does not contain the complete sanctity, for if all the settlers of Israel are not dwelling on the land then there are no obligations concerning tithing. These two entities form a unique unit. The land of Israel is sanctified with the people of Israel and the converse, Israel is sanctified by the land. There is no theory or geographical racism. The people and the land form a national religious unit that can give its complete contribution to the world civilization.[9]

Once the land is settled, the Jewish mission will be capable of fruition. If Jews exercise the land of Israel for its sacred purpose then they will demonstrate to the world community that nationalism is not an idea of lusting for power. It is a sacred concept to enhance our religion. It is a symbol only, not the essence. This is the supreme goal of Judaism that religion creates the idea of nationalism. Nationalism is only a container for religion. However with many other nations nationalism has presupposed their whole identity. Their entire historical mission has been nurtured on the state. With the Jews however, it is their religion that tells them that they must settle in a homeland. In order to foster and maintain their principles and higher goals they must have a sovereign state to perform these mitzvohs.

"So shall your children be as the stars in the heaven," declares G-d to Abraham. Only if they communicate the illumination of the Torah which is symbolic of the heavenly stars will they inherit Israel. The celestial galaxy reflects the spiritual commitment that is required of the Jewish people. The land of Israel is inherently to function on a spiritual level. It necessitates to operate only on a cultural plane. And the land shall rest on Shabbos. As Jews rest on the seventh day of the week, so must the land have a particular year wherein it rests. The Shabbos of Creation is identical with the Shabbos of the Shemita. In the Tochecha we read that the land will console itself

---

[9] *Ibid.,* p. 186.

for the many Shemitas that were defied. It is a serious transgression to forsake the Shemita year. The idea of Shemita is not to nurture the land and to protect it from erosion. The Torah has stated that if one shall ask how will we sow and how will we reap on the seventh year the answer that G-d gives is, "I will command my blessing, fulfill the land with prosperity." The Shemita denotes a spiritual rest, that the Jews must sublimate his material desires and all his yearnings for great wealth. He must transform them into spiritual goals, into a higher cultural motivating force that will enhance their national character and uplift the sanctity of the nation.[10]

G-d stood aside as it were and measured the earth and declared the land of Israel for the Jewish people. As G-d reserved the Torah for His people, for the Jewish people, likewise did He reserve a land wherein these principles could be nurtured and developed, a land that would serve as a container for the Torah. Torah must be developed in a cultural environment that is able to blossom forth with its spiritual elements and cultural factors. The Torah cannot be developed in a vacuum. It must have a land, a people, a nation. And G-d saw that this land would fall to the Jews as an inheritance. G-d bequeathed this chosen land to His chosen people who sought the Torah. That is why G-d declared His favorite land to His favorite people.

The land of Israel has its special character. If the Jews have sinned the land expels and reviles its citizens. Unlike the people of other nations who when they are cast off from their homeland upon entering another land find themselves quite at home. The Jews are not only expelled from their territory but also suffer greatly in exile for the Jewish people are the children of G-d. Hence their reward and the punishment differs from that of the other nations. The Jewish people must account for their transgressions in a more intensified form because they have a closer relationship with G-d. Hence if they sin, G-d will rebuke them. The pain that they suffer must be greater for they have greatly aggravated G-d, more so than the other nations.[11]

---

[10] Isaac Jacob Reines, *Noad Shel Dimos*, p. 45.
[11] Isaac Jacob Reines, *Orah V'Simchah*, p. 87.

When the Temple was in its majestic stage the Jewish people had reached the most glorious point in their creativity. However when the Beis Hamikdash was destroyed, the adornment and beauty of Israel was disrupted and shattered. The Talmud declares in *Baba Basra*, "The Cherubim were facing each other." In another sentence it relates that the Cherubim were facing toward the House. How do we reconcile the apparent problem that on the one hand the Cherubim face the House, the Temple? When Israel is at peace and cultural serenity is in their midst then the Cherubim face one another symbolizing the beauty of Israel and the majesty of its people. However when the Cherubim face the House, there is a lack of spiritual elevation. There is a failure in the ultimate commitment to G-d. Thus the Temple was the symbol wherein Jews could recognize the progress of Jewish spiritual identity with the Almighty Creator.

Reines perceives the resettling of Israel as being intertwined with the reconstruction of the Temple. If Jews are to realize a permanent settlement in Israel and are to dwell in safety and security, then they must erect and establish a Temple. Historical tradition has borne out that Israel's cultural creativity is dependent upon the Sanctuary. When the Sanctuary was built the Jewish pride was uplifted and its maesty was heightened to extreme loftiness. When the Holy Temple was desecrated then the Jewish people lost their glory and were cast into exile as we have seen in the destruction of two Temples. Thus resettlement of Israel must be predicated upon the fact that Jews must also establish once again a Temple in Jerusalem[12]

Man's expression of life is determined by his striving for completion and perfection. Death is indicative of corruption and the corrosive elements which lead him to decay. It is likewise with a nationality. If the people live both materially and spiritually on their own land, they are alive. However, if the nation is in exile its beauty is destroyed. The destruction of the Holy Temple made a singularly striking impression on the history of Israel. It had a crucial effect upon the Jewish

---

[12] Isaac Jacob Reines, *Or Chodosh Al Zion*, p. 81.

spirit and the Jewish vitality. Jews mourn constantly over the destruction of the Temple and are constantly reminded of it. Upon the erection of the Holy Temple Jewish nationalism will attain perfection.

If the Jewish people are to achieve their aim of aspiring to the ultimate goal of exercising the mission for which they have been chosen then they must perfect themselves spiritually. When the Jewish people reconstruct the Temple they will reclaim their majesty and glory of old.

While in exile what is the Jewish mission? It is to convey the tenets of the faith to the surrounding nations. The function of Israel in exile is to purify those who are contaminated, to elevate those who have spiritually fallen into the abyss.

The chapter in the Torah concerning the red heifer attests to this. The Midrash declares in a metaphoric passage that the burning of the red heifer symbolizes the Jewish suffering throughout the exile, throughout the dark ages, throughout the despair of the Diaspora. Finally, however, Jews will be gathered into their homeland, to the promised land of their forefathers as it is written: And a man shall gather in the ashes to a special place. The Midrash declares that G-d alone with His Glory will have to reassemble the Jews in their homeland. While in exile with all their energy they have endeavored to teach the nations of the world the ways of the Torah, ethics and morals. After having been taught they cast the Jew aside. They merely exploit the Jew, they burn the heifer and they discard the ashes. (As we have seen up till 1948.)[13]

Rabbi Akiba declares that in future time the mouth of the Jew will be filled with joy and his heart will be gladdened when Israel shall be restored to its original glory. And before they sinned, before they were decimated, Moses sang the song of Jewish redemption—*az yashir Moshe*. When the Jew will be redeemed he will sing once again. He will proclaim the wonders and miracles of G-d. Exile should only be as a temporary state of affairs and that Jews will not remain forever without a homeland. This is the dream which will be realized (has

---

[13] Isaac Jacob Reines, *Sefer Harochim*, p. 174.

been). Rabbi Akiba who was the supreme martyr, the supreme symbol of the heroic national figure was convinced that there is a future although he had witnessed Betar and Bar Cochba, the destruction of Israel's glory. Nevertheless he had faith in the future that once again Israel would resurrect itself.

How will redemption occur? How will our salvation take place? Will it be miraculous or a natural phenomenon? This question is debated among the great commentators. Many are of the opinion that the redemption will come about only through a miracle. The Ramban on *Shir Hashirim* and the Radak comment that the return to Israel will be accelerated through natural phenomena. The advent of the redemption will take place by means of man's creative ability and the independent venture by the Jewish people. Now we know also in the Zohar the sentence, "Send me away," declares the angel, "for the morning star has arisen." The Zohar comments that the morning salvation and the bright star of redemption for Israel will occur slowly, through a gradual process. We have an apparent contradiction for in Amos we read: As in the days of your exodus from Egypt so shall I perform wondrous miraculous feats for you—denoting the return to Israel. How do we reconcile the apparent paradox? Since so many scholars as the Ramban, the Radak, Zohar have attempted to define the return to Israel by natural means we must endeavor to understand the rationale behind their opinion. We must however declare that redemption must come about by man's own attempt to create an atmosphere of independence. As we have seen, the wave of nationalism has created a great sympathy for the return to Israel. Judaism will become resurrected in Israel through natural means. However when it will be realized it will be experienced as though a miracle had happened. Nature and supernatural phenomena will merge. The way of G-d will make the supernatural appear in a matter-of-fact way. The manner of G-d is to show His great glory through man's own productivity and creativity. Man must create on his own and exert all the energy which he possesses to be ultimately committed to the

---

[14] Isaac Jacob Reines, *Shnei Hamoros*, p. 38.

ideal of return to Israel and rebirth of the homeland. When the Jewish people risk their lives and dedicate their souls for Israel then will G-d's miraculous intervention appear. Nature on behalf of man, that is man's own productivity and G-d's supernatural method the *hasgacha* will merge. The Jew and G-d have the covenant of old.[15]

Reines envisages a hope that the nations of the world will examine the Jewish situation and express their willingness and desire that the Jewish people should resettle their land. We have seen this come to pass in our present time in 1947. Why shouldn't there be noble Gentiles who are endowed with the spirit of a more ethical behavior? Why shouldn't they help to contribute to create a Jewish state? We know that there have been many pious men among the Gentiles, for example, Cyrus who was called G-d's anointed one. Why in our times shouldn't there arise men who are gifted to realize that Jews must resettle their homeland and the Jewish people should fulfill their higher destiny and supreme mission on the promised land that was sworn to their forefathers? The Jewish nation is only in temporary exile, an exile that will lead to ultimate redemption. We are not resolved to an everlasting and permanent domicile in the Diaspora. The hope of the Jew is to realize his destiny on Israel's territory.[16]

Reines distinguishes between the exodus of Egypt and the present interest and concern for return to Israel. In Egypt the function of the Jews was exodus, an escape from Egypt, from servitude and bondage. Egypt did not allow them to travel beyond its borders. In our time they would graciously grant us permission to leave. However the Jews must find a homeland where they will be secure in settling it. The function of the exodus was *yetzia*. This was the main miracle that occurred. In our time the miracle must be *kenisa*.[17]

The remembrance of the exodus from Egypt is inscribed in the minds of the Jew and is everlasting in their memories

---

[15] Isaac Jacob Reines, *Sefer Harochim*, p. 90.
[16] *Ibid.*
[17] *Ibid.*, p. 91.

because it gives them encouragement to maintain themselves and to survive amidst the peril and persecution that engulf their lives. Throughout the travail of their historic existence Jews have always kept in mind the idea of redemption. This idea is characterized exclusively in the exodus of Egypt. There was seen G-d's splendor. In time of persecution and perplexity Jews recollect the great moment in history which gave them the vitality to exist and inspires them to proceed amidst the present danger of the secular environment that tends to assimilate and obliterate the Jewish consciousness. In future times when Israel will finally be redeemed Jews will no longer resort to the memory of Egypt, and of the exodus. Jews will have the final redemption and Israel will no longer have need of memories of old for Jeremiah swears in the name of G-d that there will be days to come that you will no longer remember when you went out of Egypt but you will remember G-d who redeemed you from the great exile, from the horrible holocaust. This is G-d whom you will remember. Jews will no longer need signs on the pathways toward their homeland to remind them that they must keep alive the burning embers of redemption. The final redemption will give the Jewish people that security of self-complacency on their homeland to enjoy themselves fully and to be rewarded finally for their endurance in exile and travail throughout the millennium of misery.[18]

The redemption from Egypt although it had splendid miracles and was accomplished through a miraculous feature nevertheless was imperfect. The reason for this is because the Jewish people had to suffer many exiles from their land. However the final redemption will be perfect and Israel will forever remain upon its land. The prophet declares, "He shall endure us through the two days." The Radak comments on the two exiles *V'Yom Hashlishi* and on the third day, meaning when the time will come for the final redemption the Jews will remain forever upon their promised land. The Jews who will be redeemed shall come to Zion rejoicingly with an everlasting joy. They will no longer fear the problems and perils of the Galuth. They

---

[18] *Ibid.*, p. 287.

will be filled with joy and exuberant with the idea of return. When they will experience this everlasting joyous time they will no longer feel any sense of tragedy for *simcha* terminates and negates any feeling of sorrow and remorse. Their everlasting joy will eradicate the great travail and agony which they suffered up till this present time. As long as the *Galuth,* the persecution of the exile thickens and becomes burdensome for the Jews, must they gird themselves and become encouraged that redemption is nigh and salvation, close.

This Congress (Reines referring to the Zionist Congress) is a true testimony that the idea of Zionism is not dead. It is burning the wood of the Jew, and is ever-present in our daily activities. Jews are imbued with the idea of return and aspire daily that it will be realized and they reap the fruits of their labors.[19]

When G-d shall return the captives of Zion, all the nations of the world will declare that this nation has truly endured and is worthy of its blessed land. All the civilizations of the world will come to realize that the Jewish civilization excels with its culture, that the Jewish people, who have endured and suffered so long, who have experienced so much persecution and who have sown in tears, have finally been able to reap in joy. The millennium of tragedy will be transcended into the coming millennium of Messianism. The salvation will blossom forth steadily and although Jews face many problems and are confronted by many challenges nevertheless it is a sign that this Council, namely Mizrachi, will prevail and the Jewish people will realize the state of Israel once again.

There are many concepts which are fundamental to the idea of any national sovereign people. First of all there must be a race, a family of people to perpetuate themselves. Then there must be a language and a religion to foster the cultural ideas that pertain to the particular nation. Finally there must be country, a geographical location to contain and protect the particular nation. The former concepts, namely race, language and religion are internal to the structure of a nationality. The

---

[19] Isaac Jacob Reines, *Sharay Orah.* p. 17.

country, the land where the nation should settle is external to its survival. However there is one attribute that the land or the geographical location has which is over and above the internal concepts. That is, it protects and contains the former three. Race, language and religion are essential and instrumental in the development of a creative nation. The Jewish people must have a place, a resting point wherein the concepts of nationality can be nurtured, developed and grown. The Jewish religion is the central core of its existence. The very essence of Judaism and its survival is dependent upon the performance of the entire Torah. The Jewish people must observe scrupulously and diligently all the precepts pertaining to the fulfillment of their religious obligations.

A people is constituted upon two factors, namely religion and nationality. They are inextricably intertwined and interwoven. Belief in the Torah must be interlocked with belief in the return to Israel. Only then can Jews experience the true goal of fulfilling their national destiny and unique mission that has been transmitted on Mount Sinai.

The spirit of Israel and the Jewish people becomes strengthened and hardened when the nations of the world oppress and threaten its survival. As the whips become sharper and the smitings become fiercer Israel's belief becomes ever stronger. The idea of nationalism is not bound up with a rope of silver or gold that is only external in nature. Jewish ties to their national ideal is internal, idealistic and with a supreme goal and elevated mission to achieve and to perform. A fundamental concept of the Jewish religion and cardinal point in its belief system is that a return to Israel is indispensable to the continuity of the Jewish people. All the suffering that has taken place and all the travail that has been experienced points to an ultimate return. Jews must be filled with the hope and realization that they will ultimately fulfill the everlasting dream of the rebirth and resettlement of their homeland.

To surrender this belief in the return to Israel is the abandonment of the religion because no religion can exist without a homeland. All hope is dependent upon Israel. One of the fundamental questions that man is asked when he enters the world to come is: Did you hope for salvation? Did you aspire for redemption? *tzepitah liyeshuah* Inherent in this question is a fundamental principle of the religion that Jews must always hope and be alert to the fact that salvation is nigh. The word *tsefitah* hoping is semantically identified with looking, imagining and they are interrelated. When one aspires to an ideal he visualizes it in front of him and he forms in his mind the picture of his hope that is real in essence and not merely a figment of his imagination. Prepare yourself for redemption then G-d will make you into a nation which thrives and is vibrant because belief in redemption is the necessary prerequisite for actual redemption. You must be convinced in a firm manner that the Jews will finally be redeemed and then G-d will redeem us. Jews must have the assurance and confidence that they can be redeemed. Only then will they come close to the realization of redemption.[20]

The hope of restoration in the promised land of Israel gives that vitality and affords the assurance not to submit to the forces of assimilation, not to surrender to the power of secular persuasion. All the trying efforts of the Gentile nations to assimilate and to obliterate Jewish culture shall not prevail. The Jewish people will maintain their identity in the face of all danger because their hope for the future will guide them in the present. The future blessings will serve as a remedy for the present suffering that the Jews are enduring.

Originally after the fall of the Holy Temple efforts were made to reconquer the glory of Israel, to reestablish its sovereignty. However after long and trying attempts they saw that Israel's national state could no longer survive. The hope of once again attaining the glory that was formerly had, was always kindled in the heart of each and every Jew. All the pogroms and persecutions could not extinguish the burning hope and the yearning desire to reestablish themselves in their homeland. The hope of restoration was a soothing ointment for all the suffering in exile. It furnished the Jew with the spirit to

---

[20] Isaac Jacob Reines, *Sharay Orah V'Simchah*, p. 15; *Or Chodosh Al Zion*, p. 62.

survive and it healed many a wound. It gave him the *raison d'être* that would preserve him throughout the dense darkness that befell him.[21]

The hope for restoration is not merely a great principle in its own right. It is the protector of the entire spiritual destiny. It gives vitality for the entire Torah living existence. It is the defender of the Jewish spiritual honor and the guardian of Jewish cultural glory. To those who only believe in a natural resurrection of the state, why should we throw stumbling blocks in their way and why shouldn't we assist them even though they do not believe in the type of return to which we are firmly committed, namely a redemption—a *Geulah*—of a miraculous nature? Why shouldn't we encourage them that *Geulah*, redemption, on a natural plane is also vital? We should merge these two opinions and one should complement the other in order to arrive at a truly religious community. We must harmonize and merge the secular with the sacred, not viewing them as conflicting with one another but as crescive in their polarity.

My soul is to G-d and of those who watch for Him in the morning, to those who arise before the morning star begins to dawn and await for G-d's salvation, to those my soul belongs. When a person is unsure of his salvation, he has doubts and fears certain obstacles in his path. He is not apt to show diligence in his worship and he experiences a feeling of laxity in his observance. The person who is certain that redemption will arrive will usually precede the morning star and rise like a lion to be the faithful guardian of the law and the watchman for G-d's salvation. The Jews cannot disassociate themselves from this great and historic movement, namely the Zionist movement. Nor are they free to declare that they should hide their heads in seclusion to turn aside from the great current of Zionist nationalism. Jews should rather accept this as a great spiritual movement. Indeed, every nationalist movement and every nation is spirited and encouraged by its state. The idea of nationalism develops the spirit of its nation and the idea of a state provides

---

[21] Isaac Jacob Reines, *Or Chodosh Al Zion*, p. 108.

for security and well-being that encourages and stimulates intellectual creative thought.[22]

And G-d told Abraham, "You shall know and be aware of the fact that your children shall be strangers in a land which does not belong to them." Israel's destiny in the Diaspora is always to remain a stranger. The Jews will never assimilate to the secular milieu and to the cultural environment about them. They always remain as strangers maintaining their identity in the face of perilous odds. Just as a plant needs a particular environment to grow and to be nurtured, for a plant may grow in one place and wither in another, so Israel will never assimilate because it will retain its own culture. Many factions in Judaism have sought the way of assimilation. They have tried and attempted many times to emulate the Gentile and to imitate his ways. This cannot be. It never has been and it never will be. All their attempts to associate and interrelate with the Gentile to lose their identity and to be considered the same have brought about even more wrath on the part of the Gentile. The Jews have seen time and again that when they choose to assimilate and seek security in the larger society, in the other group, instead of achieving their ultimate they invoke anger and fury.[23]

Secular Germany is the true test that answers this question. Whenever the Jew attempts to assimilate, the Gentile looks around and sees that he will lose his whipping boy. Then he lashes out against the Jews with an even greater fury because their destiny in the exile is to remain estranged and aloof from the civilization about them. The Jews will maintain their identity and guard their heritage and always remaining strangers as G-d told Abraham in the covenant that your people will remain distinct, segregated and isolated from the environment into which they have been cast. Then G-d will recount his promise of old and take into consideration the persecution and immense suffering which the Jews have incurred and then with

---

[22] Isaac Jacob Reines, *Orah V'Simchah*, p. 66.
[23] Isaac Jacob Reines, *Sharay Orah V'Simchah*, p. 38.

His grace and kindness He will once again reestablish and reconstruct the birthplace of the fatherland in Israel.

In these nations you shall never find a true resting place nor a secure home for your footstool. You will always remain segregated, different and distinct. "In our time," declares Reines, "there are people, in fact there is a movement, to assure and encourage the Jewish people to obtain equal citizenship, equal rights with the Gentile." "This," contends Reines, "is fallacious. When Jews try to ingratiate themselves in the eyes of the Gentiles they always find much bitter water in the end. Whenever Gentiles decided to grant the Jews certain privileges we know that it only lasted a short time. Then it terminated and even greater persecution ensued." Therefore the Jews must not seek to lose their identity in order to gain the security of the non-Jew. Equal rights though it seems blissful has however a bitter result. The Jew loses his identity and surrenders his tenacity for his heritage. G-d loves the gates of Zion more so than all the dwelling places of Jacob. All the dwelling places that lead to Zion, that have their focus directed towards Israel and have their roots pointed towards the development of the state of Israel, are loved by G-d and are endeared to Him and are cherished by Him much more so than those who dwell in safety and security in the Diaspora. Those who feel smug and self-complacent in the Diaspora should be aware of the fact that these pleasant winds can blow over quite quickly. The sun in whose material warmth and splendor they bask will soon disappear because it is only a temporary splendor and then the wrath of persecution will mount even higher.

The only refuge point for the Jew is Zion. This is what G-d desires and this is what He demands from us. We shall open our hearts towards the gate of Zion and close our eyes to the lusting passion of security and self-complacency that seeks to disrupt and disintegrate the Jewish people.[24]

The ninth day of Ab is the symbol of national calamity. On that day Jews commemorate the memorial of the severance from their homeland. That is the day when the national sovereignty

---

[24] Isaac Jacob Reines, *Or Chodosh Al Zion,* p. 24.

was destroyed and Jews have been thrust into exile, cast upon foreign waters to become almost submerged in the sea of suffering. The Jewish people have almost been swept away by the tides of terror and the currents of corrosion.

We can readily see how many small nations are beginning to revive their national heritage and renew their national sovereignty. The Jews who have been suffering for these two millennium go on without any interruption. This must be remedied. This is the role of the Jew, to rehabilitate the nation and to resurrect the people in their homeland. So, the ninth day of Ab brings about the solemn tragic feeling within the heart of every Jew and stirs his emotional passion for Israel and his spiritual fervor for the Holy Land. Perhaps Jews can derive the lesson from this tragedy to gather their forces and strengthen themselves to fulfill the mission of their two thousand year dream.

This day that is commemorated, namely *Tisha B'Ab* is the symbol that Jewish nationalism is still alive, that the Jewish spirit still hovers and the national feeling is ever-burning within Jewish souls. If Jews still can commemorate such a day after so many centuries of suffering it is a valid sign and a true symbol that there is hope yet for that day when redemption shall no longer be a dream and salvation will no longer be thought of as a mere vision. The Jews will envisage the reality of the restoration in their homeland.

The tears that are shed on *Tisha B'Ab* are a true expression of the yearning and love for Israel. After all the millennium of misery and centuries of tragedy Jews will cry and wail over Zion. This is truly remarkable and indeed amazing that the sparks of hope are still glowing. Only something that is dead ceases to have any emotion. The very fact that it is ever present in thought demonstrates that Zion is still alive and Israel is vibrant.[25]

There are many theorists who have suggested that Israel will assimilate. Many secularists are of that opinion. They are filled with foolishness, for many times intellectuals have thought that

---

[25] Isaac Jacob Reines, *Noad Shel Dimos*, p. 27.

Judaism has no chance for survival and would perish. However the Hand of G-d intervenes and G-d's supervision remains supreme throughout all the generations of historical travail.

"Set up for yourselves signs and symbols," declares Jeremiah, "to remember the path from where you have been driven." Only someone who plans to return can fix within his mind marks of memory. These bitter tears that were shed on the ninth day of Ab are the signs and symbols that Judaism is still vibrant. Israel is still alive. The day will come when hopes and dreams will be turned into reality. The final passage of wailing on *Tisha B'Ab* is chanted in this tone. Wail over Zion as a young woman who was betrothed and lost her promised husband. The lesson that Jews have to learn after all the bitter tears that have been shed and after all the outpourings of contrite hearts over the destruction and ruin of Zion is that there is still hope and the dream is still kindled within the Jewish soul.[26]

It is not a wailing over someone who is dead or a wailing of termination that a planned mission and goal has come to an end. It is not a mourning of finality. It is a temporary mourning, temporary grief and temporary sorrow. The young maiden is embittered over the loss of her lover and she weeps bitterly. Nevertheless, she still has hope that after the year of sorrow and regret she will attempt to find another husband. The Jews likewise have that feeling within them that hope has not been extinguished and that their dream may yet become a reality. As long as Israel considers herself like the young maiden, Jews can become inspired with the spirit of fulfilling their historic mission.

Israel will remember that these tears will turn into drops of dew from which its nationalism will be resurrected and revived and it will once again assume its proud role among the nations of the world.[27]

The nature of a person is such that he soon forgets the deceased members of his family. G-d endowed man in such a way

---
[26] *Ibid.*, p. 28.
[27] Isaac Jacob Reines, *Sefer Harochim*, p. 228.

that he shouldn't always be filled with mournful thoughts. Man's tendency is to involve himself with living problems, problems that have yet to be solved, problems that still have signs and symbols of hope. If Jews are so dedicated to their spirit of nationalism then it is a true symbol that the Jewish nation is still alive. Consoling Israel is the vision of the Prophet Isaiah in the classic chapter: "Console ye, console ye, My nation, shall declare G-d." It does not say—declared G-d—in the past tense but the future is indicated. Throughout the entire historical travail and throughout the millennium of misery Jews have endured a period of mourning, a period of suffering, anguish and tragedy. However, alongside of and accompanying this comes G-d's consolation, G-d's mercy and G-d's warmth. G-d will declare in future time that He has consoled Israel. Speak to the heart of Jerusalem for its suffering has terminated and its long misery has finally ended. Consolation of Jerusalem and Israel in every generation is an ever-present sign that the state of Israel is still alive in spirit and that the Jewish people have a sincere hope of restoring their homeland. This consolation is not one reserved for something that is dead and to one who is bereaved by a calamity that can no longer be remedied. This consolation is of another nature. It is a consolation of the future that there is still a dawn of glory beyond the dark night and Israel will arise once again to assume its original place among the nations of the world. Therefore the Prophet speaks in the future that for all times when Israel is suffering and is enduring strife Jews should keep in mind this prophecy. Whenever Jews feel the pain they should remind themselves that the cure is imminent that they will extricate themselves from the plight of exile.[28]

Rabbi Gamaliel observed a woman who had lost her young son. The woman wept bitterly. Rabbi Gamaliel who lived in her neighborhood wept alongside of her and he cried with such bitter tears that his eyelashes fell out. The homily continues that Rabbi Gamaliel wept and reminded himself of the destruction and desecration of the Temple, how the great pride and

---

[28] *Ibid.*, p. 236.

luster of Jewry was transformed into shame and abomination, how the national glory was turned into national sorrow. A great lesson can be learned from Rabbi Gamaliel. He wept at first for the young child who had passed away. This weeping soon led to the weeping for the general community. It was not merely a particularized one. It included a weeping for the *klal,* for the community. Every man when he weeps or is joyful should not only be concerned with his own welfare or be immersed in his own sorrow but his concern should encompass the welfare of the community and his sorrow should be an integral part of the anguish felt and experienced by the total community. We do not only live for ourselves. Jews must be completely involved in the community, with their own social community, not merely to have their own interests in mind however pure they may appear. Jews must endeavor to transform and elevate their personal emotions to accommodate and include them in the general welfare and in the general emotions of the community at large.[29]

He who has the patience and endurance to mourn and wail over the destruction of Jerusalem will be worthy of the precious *zechus* of seeing Jerusalem in its restoration and experiencing her glory. However one who does not involve himself in the grief and sorrow of his nation shall never see Jerusalem in its true glory. He shall never experience it for G-d will cut him off, G-d will sever him from the community of Israel. One who does not feel the pain and suffering of his people does not have the privilege to enjoy the joy and glory of his people, *midah k'neged midah.*[30]

The freethinkers who are greatly instrumental in the resurrection of the new idea of rebuilding Israel should not be discarded and cast aside by the orthodox Jews. Orthodoxy should seek the opportunity of bringing them closer to G-d and to associate and collaborate with them in strengthening the movement, for this movement of national restoration shall turn them from their mundane material pleasures and trans-

---

[29] Isaac Jacob Reines, *Noad Shel Dimos,* p. 67.
[30] *Ibid.,* p. 69.

form and elevate them to the mountain of G-d's House. The Rabbis interpret, *"Vayehi erev Vayehi boker"* as "It was nightfall, it was morning, behold it was one day." The night symbolizes the acts of the wicked, the day symbolizes the acts of the righteous. One day G-d declares that on Yom Kippur, the Day of Atonement, is a day for all wherein all unite and cleave together. The people who are considered as freethinkers and transgressors of many precepts of G-d's Torah should be given an opportunity for atonement. They should be unified with the *Zaddikim*. Everyone will readily agree that the Day of Atonement is one of supreme holiness and complete majesty, of recognizing G-d's grandeur. Nevertheless, Jews unify and solidify themselves with all ranks of the Jewish people, with the entire gamut of class and structure which is prevalent in Jewish society. Jews repent alongside of all those who are freethinkers. It is a day of unity, a day of solemn solidarity. The movement of Israel should be examined with this very approach, that it should bring unity and harmony to all Israel and not discord and disunity. Hence as the Day of Atonement symbolizes spiritual solidarity, likewise Zionism should be the emblem of cultural cohesion.[31]

The Festival of Lights, Hanukah, demonstrates the Jewish determination to uphold the national pride and to fight desperately to maintain the national identity. The heroic feats of the Hasmoneans who sacrificed their lives to protect the security of Jewish sovereignty and to defend the welfare of the people are ever crystallized in the minds of all Jews. Jews must remind themselves always of the heroic feats of the Hasmoneans for they were ready, willing and able to sacrifice themselves for the purpose of upholding and maintaining the national dignity and national glory. This dignity and glory was transmitted through the ages and even the secular world marvels at the heroic accomplishments of the Maccabees. This emotional spirit, should be aroused and inspired in each Jew that he may also relive the heroic days of the Maccabees in our time for now there are also avenues that may lead to the renewal of the homeland.[32]

---

[31] Isaac Jacob Reines, *Or Chodosh Al Zion*, p. 92.
[32] *Ibid.*, p. 93.

The Jew does not become dismayed when he is confronted with troubles, misery, and pogroms for hope is the essential quality that routinizes his stability to that degree that all external and internal suffering becomes dissipated in its sight. When he dreams of hope and envisages it before his eyes all fear of disillusion and disappointment evaporates.

Zion, won't you ask for the well-being of your enchained ones? A feeling of remorse is not sufficient to arouse or stimulate the true commitment and real dedication for Israel. It can come only from an internal emotion. It can only spring forth from *regesh* that is internalized.

*Siddurim* are replete with passages concerning feelings for Zion and Jerusalem. Jews weep constantly over the downfall of their national glory. They should not be concerned with empty weeping but must channel their emotions to that drive and direction which will guide them and give them the courage to lead themselves from the darkness of exile to the light of Zion. From the day that you have departed from Egypt shall I evince great miracles. That the coming of the new commonwealth and the new redemption will be through a miraculous and marvelous feat is not to be denied. However this does not preclude exerting all energy and motivation to lead the way and to prepare the path for a new Israel. The internalized emotion that has been discussed can be directed toward a goal that will bring to fruition the state of Israel.

When all energy has been expended, the miracle will take place. G-d's glory and grace will then shine. Hope and trust in G-d should not be predicated on supernatural intervention but the hope and courage that is sought in G-d should aid and stimulate the Jewish people to find new means whereby they can create a state that could function on the level which would make Jewry more distinguished and more glorious. In this way Jews can also contribute to the world civilization and take their place in the community of nations. Some think that Jews should only place their trust in G-d and not seek any outside or external means or natural modes to foster the Zionist movement. However, these people are only few in numbers but are men of great excellence. It is difficult to conceive of an entire nation just existing purely on the idea of hope alone. Jews must channel the concept of hope and the idea of courage to meaningful action that will create a living and viable state.[33]

Not only is it permissible for Jews to seek material means to hasten and quicken the redemption but it is incumbent upon them to seek out means that will lead to the arrival of the redemption. Jews do not need to surrender themselves completely to hope and to wait solely for the awakening from above. They should do all that is possible to hasten the goal of redemption to alleviate and to stem the tide of rampant assimilation. In order to curtail the rate of intermarriage and the disintegration of the Jewish people they must establish a national state wherein they will be proud of their Jewish heritage.

The foundation of the Torah lies in Israel and the centrality of its existence and observance is dependent upon the settling and reestablishment of Israel. The Ramban comments that all the *mitzvohs* of the Torah even though they are not contingent upon the land of Israel are nevertheless to be observed primarily in Israel. The reason that they are performed beyond the territory of Israel is only to give knowledge and preparation to fulfill them when in the Holy Land.[34]

A Jew should always seek to make his domicile in Israel. He who lives beyond the borders of Israel is considered to be an idolator. The Rabbis declared that living in Israel is a great virtue and they considered its importance to be of inestimable value. They recognized the worth and import inherent in living in Israel, that it would imbue the person with the spirit of his nation and the soul of his people. The Rabbis also felt that living in Israel would inspire and give one a holy aspect of his life. Therefore, one should endeavor to make his domicile in Israel to create, nurture and develop himself culturally and to give himself the background necessary to maintain his spiritual survival.

The commandment of settling Israel, though incumbent

---

[33] Isaac Jacob Reines, *Sharay Orah V'Simchah*, p. 8.
[34] Werfel, *op. cit.*, p. 361.

upon us and though Jews are required to fulfill it, has great value and is a prerequisite for maintaining the national cultural heritage. Whether we agree that the *mitzvah* of settling in Israel is biblical in nature or whether we concur that it is only rabbinical, is immaterial. However, its efficacy in influencing the course of history is not altered. The settling of Israel is the *mitzva* perhaps which is singular in its unique quality of merging both emotion and reason. Most of the commandments are singular in nature and private in scope. However settling of Israel is that *mitzvah* which is total in scope. It embraces the entire Jewish community and everyone should be aroused and animated with the purpose and wish of fulfilling the goal of resettlement. If settling in Israel is a commandment, naturally the method of settling there should also be considered a commandment. If Jews are commanded to capture Israel then capturing it by military force is also a commandment. Jews should not be passive rather they must be active in their commitment to Israel. One may also resort to the means of buying land in Israel for it, too, is vital and Jews need not acquire Israel by military force if it can be acquired through peaceful means. Buying land in Israel is extremely important in the resettling of it and everyone should participate with his heart and soul, body and mind to achieve the purpose of resettling Israel.[35]

According to the Ramban there are two integral parts that are interrelated concerning the *mitzva* of settling Israel. First Jews must try to develop the land agriculturally and in our time also mechanically. However there is another aspect to this *mitzva,* namely to wrest the territory from the Gentile and the heathen. That Israel shall be inherited by the Jews denotes the idea that they must be in complete ownership of its land. Jews alone are the sole owners and guardians of their territory. Only Israel, only the Jewish people shall inherit and conquer this territory, for it is to their fathers and to them that G-d has promised and bequeathed this land.

Upon your walls, Jerusalem, have I appointed watchmen, guardians of the faith and heritage. These guardians are the

---

[35] Isaac Jacob Reines, *Or Chodosh Al Zion,* p. 49.

souls of men and their yearnings are for arriving at the idea of creating a state of Israel. In every Jew there is latent the power to expose from within himself his creative capacity for rebuilding Israel. In every person is revealed the mystery of his own spiritual energy and he only has to activate himself and express it in concrete and definitive terms. The Rabbis expound on the sentence the You shall arise and have mercy on Zion. Another Rabbi declared, "You, O G-d, shall rebuild Jerusalem" for when the Jewish people shall arrive at the idea that Israel must be rebuilt and restored then Jews say to G-d that He must aid them. He must deliver the Jewish people and He must be their salvation. This phrase in Isaiah concludes, "Do not give any rest to him." This means that Jews should not desist from the idea of resurrecting Israel for it is incumbent and binding upon every Jew to realize his own salvation in the state of Israel. Everyone must be aware of the fact that tilling the soil and plowing the land is a function that is mutually related to the fulfillment of many *mitzvos.*

As has been noted, taking tithes is only contingent upon the land of Israel, that is it can only be prevalent in Israel. However there are other precepts that are affiliated with the idea of agriculture, namely all the festivals which are concerned with the *regel,* ascending to Jerusalem. Passover, Shavuoth and Succoth are all associated in some form with the idea of agriculture. That is, Jews sanctify agriculture sublimate and transcend the plain and simple labor of tilling the soil by transforming it into a high ideal, working toward the commitment for a holy land. The holiday expresses the idea that work in the land should be sanctified. It has a specific function to elevate man and to give him a purpose and direction on this earth.[36]

The Torah abhors taking usury and detests lending money for interest, for it deprives man of the basic pleasure of working diligently and industriously at his labor. The receiving of interest is a fruitless manifestation of a parasitic type who leeches upon his fellow man and expunges him of all his material wealth. This is not the preoccupation and main concern of the

---

[36] Werfel, *op. cit.,* p. 362.

Torah. The Torah is basically concerned with an idealistic way of living, a way of enjoying man's fruitful labors. Hence the Torah elevated man's work and placed the idea of labor in a high plane. "Love work," is declared in the "Ethics of the Fathers."

Reines relates how he was elated at the emergence of the new movement. The Zionist movement was establishing settlements in Israel where business was being transformed into sickles. The chicanery of commercial living was turned into the nobility of tilling the soil. However he grew despondent for he observed that many thousands of Jewish families were leaving Europe and settling in America. He felt anger and remorse for he was convinced that these families would be destined for assimilation. The families who left Europe for America went to settle on the other side of the Atlantic and they also settled beyond the borders of cultural Judaism. They should have settled in Israel to increase the productivity and output of the new settlement. "We should be concerned," declares Reines, "about these families who are leaving the cultural milieu of Judaism in order to become more westernized and more modernized in the New World." The two opposing camps who have sharp and radical views concerning the resettling of Israel have sought to advance much strife and a great deal of aggravation among the Jewish people. The freethinkers and the intellectuals who are of the opinion that Jews must build Israel completely on their own and that they must resort only to *teva,* to natural means of rebuilding have incurred the enmity of those who are ultra-orthodox. The ultra-orthodox on the other hand believe that Jews should not make any innovations on their own. They should wait until G-d with His glory reveals Himself and redeems the Jewish people from bondage.[37]

The two opposing views have many fallacies within them. They are both extreme in their point of view. Much enmity has been created because of these sharply opposing views. Jews must seek to blend and harmonize the two. That is, Israel must be rebuilt by natural means. The Jewish people must try to the

---

[37] *Ibid.,* p. 363.

utmost of their ability to produce on their own as much as possible. However, this should not preclude the hope and aspiration that G-d in His glory will reveal His miraculous and wondrous ways. Jews must harmonize and synthesize the two. Only then can they realize the rebuilding of Israel. If Jews do not invest any time, effort or energy in the rebuilding of Israel then it is a sign that there is no life in the Jewish community. In short, G-d helps those who help themselves.

Jews should not be dismayed if the nations of the world view them with contempt and intolerance. Gentiles consider Jews as strangers without a country, as people who are odd and mysterious. Hence they disparage and revile the Jew. However in our times we see that Jewish feeling of national dignity and cultural pride is ever vibrant and dynamic. It is only externally throughout the ages that Jews have lost their national pride and dignity. When the spirit of nationalism has reawakened we observe how the Jewish community is alert and aware to mobilize all its forces and solidify all its strength for the purpose of creating a sovereign state. Therefore Jews pray on the High Holy Days, "G-d, Grant glory to Your people." The nations of the world shall revere and appreciate the Jewish nation. Jewish people pray that it shall become revealed that they have not lost their sense of pride and the nation of Israel is yet dignified in stature and its mission of being a leader among the nations will yet be realized.[38]

Reines is disappointed and concerned about the newly established settlement and why it has not been broadened and enhanced three or fourfold times as much as it is in the present state. Every Jew, contends Reines, should be filled with joy and his heart should be gladdened for in Israel is seen the refuge point and the sanctuary of Jewish salvation. Many settlements have been established and many families have been able to resettle themselves in the homeland. Jews should endeavor to strengthen the settlement with more vigor and more energy, for only in Israel can be placed the assurance and only there shall be the salvation for the entire Jewish community realized.

---

[38] Isaac Jacob Reines, *Sefer Harochim*, pp. 65-66.

We really have seen the supervision of G-d in Israel, how this tiny settlement has been saved from countless pestilences and plagues, how this tiny community has managed to survive in the face of so many dangers thrust upon it. Shouldn't Jews be amazed and awestricken at G-d's grandeur and His grace that He has bestowed upon them? Those who thought originally that becoming involved with the Gentiles is the cure-all for relieving anti-Semitism were greatly mistaken. Now that they have observed that the Gentile will always revile them they return to the old concept of revering their nationalism and appreciating the dignity of the Jewish people. These people are truly repenting for they now appreciate the ideal of tenaciously clinging to tradition.

The dry bones, of whom the prophet Ezekiel prophesied, a collectivity of all the various parts, will beget a new generation. A new era dawns on Judaism when the various broken parts of all Judea shall be collected, assembled and unified. These bones symbolize the external parts of Judaism, the external structure that needs to be mended and healed. All the persecuted people from the various distant lands must be brought together, healed and cured from their ills and great suffering. However, after these bones are collected and unified there will be a signal from G-d to ignite its personality and light the spark of spiritualism. For a mere collection of the external parts of Judaism, the external structure does not suffice, since the nation must be invigorated and enlightened by the spirit. G-d will inspire the Jews to develop and enhance their national cultural heritage as He inspired and created anew the dry bones of Ezekiel.[39]

"The clouds of misery," declares Reines, "have brought together Jews from all corners of the earth to pray and reawaken themselves and yearn for Jerusalem and Zion." All the people who sought to assimilate within the cultural milieu of the secular society have begun a reawakening process. The dawn of a new era has arisen in Judaism and a new horizon begins to appear. The *Pesikta,* it will be recalled, declares that Jerusalem will become great and Israel shall extend itself. The people will

---

[39] Isaac Jacob Reines, *Shnei Hamoros,* p. 31.

come, as it were, on clouds. Reines sees the symbolism behind this, namely that the clouds of history which have darkened for a while the Jewish hopes will cluster about the Jewish people and finally when the darkness will seem to reach its densest point and all hope for salvation and redemption will be gone only then dew will begin to fall upon the earth and G-d's glory will descend upon Israel. Israel will at that time enhance itself and broaden its national scope. "No one would have believed that in our time," declared Reines, "a new arrival, a new dawn in Jewish History would occur." Jews have experienced the recent pogroms and the great travail, the great persecutions. They have rejuvenated the Jewish spirit toward a reawakening, a revival for the national cultural idea, a resurrection of the idea of the rebirth of a Jewish state. All those who assimilated and thought that there is no hope for Judaism have turned from their lethargic slumber and grasped the opportunity to once again dedicate themselves for a renewal of the nation and people.[40]

The question that arises is why now in modern times has there appeared a movement of reawakening and an organization to reestablish the national homeland in Israel. There were many periods in Jewish History in which the Jews experienced persecution, torture and humility. Why then has a new movement arisen now, in the present day? What is the significance of this new epoch-making movement in modern Jewish History? "The answer" suggests Reines, "is based upon an acute observation of Jewish History." Formerly, throughout the entire period of the Middle Ages, no matter how persecuted they were and no matter how perplexed they felt, were nevertheless imbued with the fact that G-d alone would restore them to their original glory. They felt that their sins, iniquities and transgressions brought upon them the great wrath and fury of G-d. They felt that they had to cleanse and purify themselves from the contaminations with which they had been involved.

In our times they reached the other extreme, the point of no return as it were, all of a sudden like the coming of a titanic

---

[40] Isaac Jacob Reines, *Sharay Orah*, p. 26.

thunderclap, Jews have realized that there is no salvation in the Gentile, no redemption in the heathen. Hence in previous times Jews, no matter how persecuted they were, would always place their trust in G-d and nothing could shake them, nothing could move them from their close commitment and complete identification with G-d. However in our times those people who have assimilated and have been shaken from their roots of assimilation have begun to turn from the branch of the other civilization to retrieve their roots, to redirect their growth toward the reestablishment of the sovereignty of Israel.

When the Jewish people will declare that they wish to assimilate and lose their identity as Jewish people and want to find grace in the eyes of the Gentile nations, they want to cleave and intermingle with them, then G-d declares vehemently that this shall never come to be. G-d alone will be the sole Protector of Israel and the only Defender of the Jewish community.[41]

The Zionist movement is the true test which upholds and preserves the Jewish identity. This is G-d's method for stemming the tide of assimilation and Jewish disintegration. This is the manner in which G-d has revealed that Judaism shall not perish. It shall resurrect itself and return to its former glory.

This people shall dwell separate and apart from all the nations of the world. With the advent of the modern movement to disassociate the Jews from their Judaism and to mislead them into the abyss of assimilation a new method was sought to strip the Jew from his culture. This method was to declare that the Jewish people are no longer a nation, but merely a religion. Step by step their religious customs, traditions, and laws were ignored to hasten the path leading to their amalgamation with the world community. However as the fury of assimilation grew greater and greater, G-d's intervention became apparent, namely that He did not allow the Jewish people to disassociate themselves and to disenfranchise themselves from their tradition and heritage. Everyone has now observed G-d's Hand and His glory in the midst of Jewry. They will now realize even though many of them have already assimilated,

---

[41] Isaac Jacob Reines, *Sefer Harochim*, p. 150.

they will return to the fold as we have seen. This movement bears witness and is a living testimony to the fact that Jews have renewed their Jewish consciousness and have reawakened in themselves their Jewish identity. They will once again begin to value themselves as truly G-d's nation and will hold in high esteem the heritage of old. Isn't it an astounding feat and a unique phenomena that those who were completely secure in their material needs have turned from their complacency of assimilation to be at the helm of the movement which seeks to rebuild the homeland? Shouldn't we be amazed at these people, whom we had considered to be completely assimilated, who rose to become the pioneers of Israel? They no longer had any desire to pursue their pleasures, but took their belongings to travel eastward, towards Israel, the Promised Land. They knew that they would not find an abundance of food, wealth or great treasures there. They realized that they would have to relinquish their material comforts and pleasures for the ideal of Zionism. These people who were almost lost began once again to assume the role of truly idealistic Jews. It is an unusual phenomena that all the problems and the great misfortunes which the Jews have experienced have in themselves resurrected the Jewish community. These misfortunes have turned those who were evil and malevolent into Jews who are trustworthy and conscientious in safeguarding their heritage. They have transformed the transgressor and elevated him to the position of nobility. These persecutions have given the Jew the feeling of *noblesse oblige*. That is, the upper class who were secure in life's material comforts began to see the plight of their brethren and felt the need to reexamine and reevaluate their goals in life. Hence they became idealistic and began to organize this new movement of Zionism.[42]

The fundamental purpose of the recent pogroms and tragedies have an inherent cause and have albeit a mysterious motive. This is to arouse in the Jew his feeling for the homeland. It is in the foundations of repentance, repentance for the memory of Israel that Jews remember their homeland, that they

---

[42] Isaac Jacob Reines, *Sharay Orah V'Simchah,* p. 38.

will return, that they must return. This is the ethical purpose which is conveyed in the return to Israel, the ethical mission which is involved in the resurrection and rebuilding of the homeland in Israel. There is another motive involved in returning to the homeland and that is the economic welfare of brethren in the Jewish community as a whole. There is no doubt that when Jews return to Israel the standard of their brethren's welfare, economically and socially, will be immeasurably improved. The yearning that these persecutions have awakened within the Jewish community is not in vain. The Midrash in Ruth declares that when the Jewish people will return to their national homeland, they will return to G-d. They are mutually interrelated and interwoven with one another. The movement of Zionism has awakened a new response and imbued those who were completely assimilated with the idea that Judaism must survive and that the Jewish people are eternal.[43]

Every national movement is linked with a spiritual idea. There is no organization of any nationality which has no spiritual idea identified with it. However, the problem is whether the idea or spirit of a people motivates it to live in a particular geographical location or whether the geographical boundary lines are simply to provide and maintain that particular nation in an economic and materialistic manner. We may prove with regard to Israel that the main purpose of its nationality and its idea of nationhood is first and foremost of a spiritual nature. The test is demonstrable when it is recognized that even without a geographical boundary line or territorial location the Jew has still maintained his close ties and great attachment to his idea of nationalism. The idea of Zionism has never been severed from the Jewish mind. It is the very essence of Jewish life. It has already been noted that many commentaries state that all the *mitzvos* were issued primarily to be observed only in Israel. Hence we may derive from the Jewish commitment to the idea of Zionism that Jews are ultimately bound up and identified with their homeland. It is not mere fantasy but is the

---

[43] Isaac Jacob Reines, *Sefer Harochim*, pp. 115-116.

very essence of Judaism. Jews are not like the other nationalities who when they are removed from their own territorial location simply adopt the new nationality and assimilate completely with its culture as can be seen in the case of the Greeks, Romans, Persians and other great conquering nations. The Jew has never lost his identification and yearning for his homeland. Therefore with the Jew it is axiomatic to uphold the spirit of the national ideal and not merely the idea of economic productivity. We can discern from the great longing for Israel that the Jewish nationalistic idea is a spiritual one, in the true sense of the word.[44]

The Zionist idea brings close those who are removed from the spiritual center and cultural mainstream of Jewish thought and its religious ideology. It is designed to protect the Jew in the present from the rising tide of assimilation. It also has another function which is to guide Jews in the future, to lead them and bring them close to the ultimate ideal wherein they will realize the promised land of their forefathers. The Chidah writes in his book *Shem Hagdolim*, that if one, G-d forbid, loses his children he should call his next son Ben Zion. This will symbolize his identification with Zion. Reines sees in this an inherent connection with the Jew and the Zionist idea. Ben Zion, the son of Zion is a symbolic identification that brings one closer to the spiritual ideal of unification with the promised land. Only if one binds himself with the national destiny can he assure himself an everlasting name. Therefore the best *segulah* as it were for one who loses children is to call his next child Ben Zion. That will give an increased stamp of sanctity to that particular son, for he is endowed with a mission to uphold and maintain, to guard and to preserve the Jewish national cultural heritage.[45]

Reines declares, "When I entered the Zionist movement and I assumed the role of religious leader with all the responsibilities incumbent upon me, I appreciated more and more the ever-growing need and the increased dedication which is expressed

---

[44] Isaac Jacob Reines, *Or Chodosh Al Zion*, p. 59.
[45] Isaac Jacob Reines, *Sefer Harochim*, p. 69.

by the adherents of this movement. I became more appreciative and in fact my heart was filled with gratitude because I saw how people who had been completely submerged in the sea of assimilation shook off their indifference and reawakened their souls to the spiritual idea of Zionism." It is very disheartening that many Jewish leaders are discontented with the new religious movement of Zionism. It is therefore the duty and moreover a religious obligation to foster the new movement, to establish it on a firm footing, to reawaken the Jewish people for the zeal of Zionism and to inspire them with the spirituality of this great cause.[46]

The task of the Rabbi at the pulpit is immensely difficult for he faces the great opposition of those who are in the radical right. The Rabbi who is preaching for Zionism must be ever alert to offset the arguments and fallacious claims that are being expressed and argued by the orthodox rabbinate. The goal then of the book written by Reines *Or Chodosh Al Zion* has its purpose to combat the claims argued by the orthodox rabbinate. It is a systematic approach to negate and cancel the testimonies and arguments suggested to uproot the essence of this great movement. This polemical work is to establish once and for all the place of a Zionist movement within the framework of the Jewish nation. Belief in the Jewish nation is a cardinal element of the Jewish religion and they are of course mutually bound with one another. Hence the Zionist ideal is that movement created for one purpose—to resurrect the Jewish nation and thereby enhance the Jewish religion.[47]

"Emotion and truth," claim the orthodox rabbis, "are two separate functions." Jews must believe in Israel, not merely have an emotional attachment to it. Reines, however, firmly disagrees with this notion. He contends that the emotion for Israel, the love for Israel is a religious love. One cannot separate or distinguish emotional love from religious love. The two are mutually related. It is precisely those who are far removed from the spiritual core and religious mainstream of Jewish thought

---

[46] Isaac Jacob Reines, *Shnei Hamoros*, p. 32.
[47] Isaac Jacob Reines, *Or Chodosh Al Zion*, p. 74.

who embarked upon the road of rebuilding the homeland. Those who were overwhelmed and imbued with the civil liberties that were being granted to each and every Jew were at once perplexed and distraught when they experienced the pogroms of the modern era. Gratitude should be extended to their keen awareness of the national cultural revival. They have shown the path of return when they expressed their extreme willingness to rebuild the homeland. This is why they were the forerunners of the pioneer work in Israel. They are the *Chalutzim,* the builders who put their shoulders to the ground and tilled the soil with the sweat of their brow. It is to them that we owe thanks and gratitude. Should we not be perplexed and filled with wonder at this dilemma that our co-religionists who are filled with reverence for G-d have been remiss in their duty for the rebuilding of Israel and those who are far removed from religious observance are renewing with zeal the idea of Zionism? In our day when cultural Judaism has sunk to a new low and the level of cultural aspirations disintegrates daily, how can the Jewish people not look to Israel for their salvation? How can they keep still and how can they remain silent in the present day and age? Jews must review their line of reasoning and reassess the state of their culture. To progress and develop their culture is the firm goal and sincere motivating force. The eyes of the Jew must be fixed to resurrect their nation in Israel, their homeland.[48]

There are two ways of being affiliated with a group, internally or externally. We can either be affiliated internally, that is our entire being is directed and motivated in thought, deed and action in a similar fashion with the other members of the group, or externally, which is merely to have the same goals of the group but not to use similar methods of attaining them. Identification with the irreligious members of the Zionist movement is purely external. We only ally ourselves with them for the goal of the movement which is to establish a firm homeland for our oppressed brethren. However our methods and means toward establishing this movement differ widely. The Jewish

---

[48] Isaac Jacob Reines, *Sharay Orah V'Simchah,* p. 39.

people properly have a religious motivation for Israel and not a secular one. Jews are motivated by their belief in G-d not only by their emotional ties to Israel. Jews must therefore keep in mind that they may associate and it is a practical way of life to associate with these freethinkers and irreligious people. It is a daily occurrence for the Jew to associate with them in all facets of communal life and social activity. Why then should Jews not associate and work with them for this great goal to establish the homeland of Israel? Jews should even endeavor to seek an *esprit de corps* between the irreligious and the religious point of view.[49]

The Talmud relates that any communal fast that does not include the transgressors of Israel is not a valid fast day. In communal suffering and in communal tragedy Jews must take into accord all their brethren, even those who have strayed from the path of pure religious observance. Jews must take into their midst all Jews from all areas and with all points of view. This dictum symbolizes all Jews no matter how removed they are from the path of true religious observance. The irreligious must also participate in the communal suffering and the sorrow of their brethren. They must assert themselves and join together to rebuild and reestablish their homeland. The resettlement of Israel must come from people of all groups and all walks of Jewish life.[50]

There are those who contend that because the Zionist movement has leaders who are irreligious and completely removed from the main currents of religious Jewish thought these people should not be associated with them. This is a false conception based upon a misunderstood frame of reference. True, they are irreligious. However in every humanitarian movement and social organization there are bound to be those who are freethinkers and those who are religious from their own point of view. This should not preclude association with them nor should the orthodox remove themselves or segregate themselves from

---

[49] Isaac Jacob Reines, *Or Chodosh Al Zion*, p. 85.
[50] Isaac Jacob Reines, *Sefer Harochim*, pp. 150-153.

adopting the platform of this movement namely to rebuild the promised homeland to resettle the Jewish people there.

The people who have these false contentions and erroneous conceptions state that the orthodox should not be involved with them and should not ally themselves with the freethinkers in the rising Zionist movement. They are filled with fear and apprehension. This is not the Jewish way of life. It is not the orthodox approach. It is the approach of a conservative and reactionary position. It is a form of decrepit thinking, not a form of dynamic and vibrant reasoning. Therefore, orthodox Jews have to reappraise their way of life. They cannot, like the ostrich, hide their heads in the sand. They must face the present times, the present problems and cast their thoughts in a new frame of reference. Then they will be able to observe this great new movement. They will be able to give due credit to those who, even though they are removed from the religious way of life, are nevertheless concerned with the plight of their brethren.

Reines had also words of caution and rebuke to those freethinkers who consider themselves authorities in the area of Jewish education. He decried that in the area of politics the *Charedim* referring to religious Jews who are associated with the Zionist movement, do not interfere with the political structure of the movement. The religious Zionists, although many of them have great insight in the area of diplomacy, nevertheless defer to the secularists in these matters. The area of religious education, however, should be reserved for those who are authorities in this field. The task of educating youth should be delegated to those who have the know-how and background, who are equipped with the erudition and experience in teaching and guiding youth. There is still another danger involved. If the freethinkers will intrude into the educational affairs of religion, the laity will lose its trust and confidence in the new movement and its potential influence will be greatly diminished. The people will think that since the freethinkers are exceeding the boundary in religious educational matters consequently they have exceeded their authority in the total area of nationalism.

They will acquiesce to the false propaganda being issued by those who are against this great movement.[51]

Reines, though torn between his religious beliefs and his passionate love for the Jewish people however removed they were from the path of Judaism, never relinquished his zeal for the Zionist movement. He was never thwarted from the road leading to the renewal of the homeland and the renaissance of national dignity and sovereign individuality. He had a firm belief in the everlasting and timeless character of the Jewish nation. He held steadfast to his convictions, combating the opposition of the radical right and rejecting the heresy of the secular left. Both his verbal elocution and his prolific pen paved the way towards the creation of a new horizon within the scope of religious Jewry. He inspired the masses and instructed the scholars to bear the yoke and carry the torch that would guide Jews in future times. He was a man who envisaged the national historic destiny performing its unique and timeless mission on its promised soil. The idea of nationalism for him was symbolized and characterized as an avenue of spiritual communication and as a highway for transmitting the sublime cultural mission of Israel to the nations of the world.

---

[51] Isaac Jacob Reines, *Shnei Hamoros,* p. 38.

# Selected Bibliography

Berdeshevsky, Michael S., "Rabbi Isaac Jacob Reines," *Otzar Ha Sifrut*, 2, Cracow, Joseph Fisher, 1882.
Berlin, Meyer, *From Wolozin To Jerusalem, 1-2*, Yalkut, Tel Aviv, 1939-1940.
Cohen, Moshe, "Rabbi Isaac Jacob Reines," *Bamishor, I*, No. 34, Agudath Sofrim Datim, Israel, 1940.
Fishman, J. L., *Sefer Ha Yovel*, Mosad Ha Rav Kook, Jerusalem, 1946.
Gordon, J. L., "Memoirs of Rabbi Isaac Reines," *Hadoar*, No. 18 (1965), Histadrut Ivrit, New York.
Reines, Isaac Jacob, *Eduth B'Yaacov, Sermons*, Dvoretz, Vilna, 1872.
Reines, Isaac Jacob, *Chosem Tochnit*, Rom-Vilna, 1881.
Reines, Isaac Jacob, *Orim Gedolim*, Rom-Vilna, 1886.
Reines, Isaac Jacob, *Sharay Orah*, Rom-Vilna, 1886.
Reines, Isaac Jacob, *Or Shivat Ha-Yomim*, Rom-Vilna, 1896.
Reines, Isaac Jacob, *Orah V'Simchah*, Rom-Vilna, 1898.
Reines, Isaac Jacob, *Sharay Orah V'Simchah*, Rom-Vilna, 1899.
Reines, Isaac Jacob, *Or Chodosh Al Zion*, Rom-Vilna, 1902.
Reines, Isaac Jacob, *Shnei Hamoros*, S. Belechovsky-Pyetrokov, 1913.
Reines, Isaac Jacob, *Sefer Harochim*, Rabbi Isaac Jacob Publication Society, Inc., New York, 1926.
Reines, Isaac Jacob, *Noad Shel Dimos*, Solomon, Jerusalem, 1934.
Reines, Isaac Jacob, *Netzach Yisroel—Maimor Chibat Zion*, Mosad Ha Rav Kook, Jerusalem, 1937.
Reines, Isaac Jacob, *Eduth B'Yaacov*, Mosad Ha Rav Kook Jerusalem, 1951.
Shapiro, Moshe S., *Rabbi Moshe Shmuel Shapiro and His Generation*, Shapiro Brothers, New York, 1964.
Weinberg, J. J., "Rabbi Isaac Jacob Reines," *Bamishor, I*, No. 35, Agudath Sofrim Datim, Jerusalem, 1940.
Wolfsberg, Y. O., "Two Great Luminaries of Mizrachi," *Or Hamizrach*, No. 3 (1956), Mizrachi Ha Poel Ha Mizrach, New York.
Zahav, I. Gush, "Rabbi Isaac Jacob Reines," *Sheluot*, No. 7 (1952) Zionist Organization—Religious Department, Youth Activities—Jerusalem.